Present Danger

Present Danger
Towards a Foreign Policy

ROBERT CONQUEST

BASIL BLACKWELL : OXFORD

British Library Cataloguing in Publication Data

Conquest, Robert
  Present danger.
  1. Great Britain—Foreign relations—1945—
  I. Title
  327.41   DA588
  ISBN 0 631 11311 8

Typeset by Cotswold Typesetting Ltd Gloucester and
Printed in Great Britain by
Billing and Sons Ltd.
London, Guildford and Worcester

For Jon Manchip White

Contents

Preface

It is the duty of those who conduct our foreign policy to consider the details, the local opportunities and difficulties, and the immediate tactics and strategies. It is the higher duty of the political leadership to settle the general principles and the grand strategy of the nation's whole commitment in the world.

This book is not designed to solve particular problems, hardly even to present them—except to the extent that they illustrate, or are essential to, the central issues: the avoidance of nuclear annihilation on the one hand and of the subjugation of our country and culture by an alien despotism on the other.

It is with these profounder—yet more readily comprehensible —matters that I chiefly deal, declaring the main principles that appear to be necessary to the conduct of a sane and suitable foreign policy, and the main factors to be taken into account in the modern world. I hope in a later and longer work to develop many of these propositions more fully.

This book thus is not an attempt to devise systematic solutions in the realm of foreign policy, nor a blueprint by which all the complexities of the world scene may readily be mastered. It is, rather, an examination of the basic dynamics of international politics.

The chief problem today, or so I would argue, lies in the relationship between our own political culture and those quite alien to us, with their own history, attitudes, motivations; and the main danger is of applying our own assumptions to quite different mentalities and thus finding ourselves radically misunderstanding the world and conducting policies founded on fantasy. In the era of the fusion bomb and the totalist state the dangers are obvious.

Much of what is argued here is applicable to Western policy

as a whole; much is specific to the United Kingdom; and in much of what has a general Western application, the United Kingdom is in a position to give a lead.

My thanks are due to the Woodrow Wilson International Centre for Scholars, Washington, and to the Hoover Institution, Stanford, which have helped me in various ways, though they have no responsibility for the opinions expressed; and to Mrs. Moira Dawson, who assisted in the preparation of the manuscript.

Acknowledgements

Part of this material has appeared in different form in *Foreign Affairs*, *Soviet Analyst*, *Encounter*, *Policy Review*, *The New Republic*, *The National Review*, *The Daily Telegraph*, *The New Statesman*, *The American Spectator*, '*Defending America*' (introduction by James R. Schlesinger, New York 1977), and in evidence given before Committees of the US Senate and House of Representatives.

1

Facing the Eighties

The world today is complex, full of eddies and cross-currents, of local and particular issues each contributing its portion of danger and difficulty. Yet, as we all know, there is one great central question beside which the others are peripheral: can peace be kept? The answer—a potentially sinister one—is that we do not know. No absolute guarantee that nuclear war can be prevented is possible. All that we can do is to select the line of policy that most greatly reduces its likelihood.

It is conceivable that Western civilization will, after all, fail. Even barring a major war, it is not impossible that a Communist or other barbarism might extinguish liberty throughout the world, that the planet might be turned into a vast slave empire for an indeterminate length of time.

More immediately, the period ahead is likely to see an imbalance against us, both in nuclear weapons, and in expansion by the Communist powers in critical areas, unless a political and military consolidation takes place in the West.

In the Western world, and perhaps particularly in the United States and Britain, the mood of the late seventies is one, if not of frustration, at least of doubt.

In the early sixties, it was widely thought that the problems of our society, and of the world as a whole, though huge and urgent, were on the way to solution, and that the application of power and good will was all that was required to solve them.

The decade which followed was marked by a puncturing of these illusions. In Vietnam, a war entered into on liberal principles failed to achieve its ends. In the Soviet Union, the comparatively liberal rule of Khrushchev was brought to an end, and the country settled down to a period of gloomy reaction. In China, ninety-nine of the 'Hundred Flowers' were uprooted after a brief interval. In Africa the independence gained by most of the continent had varying results, not all of them reassuring; while in the southern half of the continent little progress could be observed.

The Western countries had many internal difficulties: a massive application of funds failed to solve the problems of the great cities, and a vast increase in the number of those both in secondary and higher education, together with the introduction of supposedly more advanced methods, did not produce the expected results.

We are now in a more sober mood. Our various failures have shown us that our social problems and the problems of world politics are not as easily soluble as we had thought. In many spheres we no longer believe in simple formulae which will give us a solution. But neither do we believe that any other form of society has found better solutions. Indeed, the idea that our own political culture, which is the achievement of a thousand years, can simply be scrapped no longer has much public appeal. Thoughtful men of both the Left and the Right see, that while political liberty is not in itself a solution to many problems, it at least provides the open, self-questioning milieu in which they can be tackled without replacing them by worse.

Yet, as in all such periods of disappointment, the voices of decadence and degeneration are powerful. In particular such periods are always accompanied by a loss of morale among important sections of those most sensitive to disappointment. As ever, this has shown itself in a great weakening and corruption of thought. Intellectual exhaustion has also encouraged a tendency to seek short cuts aimed at quick, radical and total solutions to problems which really need deeper analysis and more complex remedies. As Adlai Stevenson said of Korea, there are no short cuts to security: 'There are only short cuts to defeat'.

After the excessive hopes and the refractory realities of period just past, we do not want to go to the other extreme of the manic-depressive cycle. We simply need a return to sobriety. Yet the programmes offered us of late still tend to fall into two categories. There are those based on calculations of petty economic advantage; and there are those which consist of Utopian fantasy. It is time that we had something in between the two, that our vision should be concentrated neither on the

inch of mud in front of our boots nor on dreams of an impossible
zenith, but on the broad and real horizons actually before us.

The mood in the United States, both popular and governmental, now largely tends to the idea that America alone cannot
adequately cope with the problems of the world. As for British
power, confidence and prestige, these have been at a low ebb
for some years. There is no real reason to take this as permanent:
(Orwell remarks that it is mainly 'intellectuals' who think that
a trend must go on—that, as he put it, since Rommel has
reached Tobruk he is bound to reach Alexandria). One needs a
little perspective. When American friends offer condolences on
Britain's situation, I answer that we have had these bad moments
before—in the reigns of Henry VI and Charles II, for example.

The Times lately condemned what it saw as a current
'nostalgia for Empire' in certain circles. If it meant that anyone
contemplates with even the remotest seriousness any restoration
of colonial rule, this would be nonsense (even George III
accepted the *fait accompli* in America with good grace). Yet
Dean Acheson's view that 'Britain has lost an empire and has
not yet found a role' retains some truth. Whatever may be
said of the old imperial system, it both gave the British an
international attitude of mind and established a deep tradition
of responsible administration, trade and education on the world
scale. The sudden reversion to a rather empty local materialism
has been well expressed by the poet Philip Larkin in his 'Homage
to a Government':

> Next year we are to bring the soldiers home
> For lack of money, and it is all right.
> Places they guarded, or kept orderly,
> Must guard themselves, and keep themselves orderly,
> We want the money for ourselves at home
> Instead of working. And this is all right.
>
> It's hard to say who wanted it to happen,
> But now it's been decided nobody minds.
> The places are a long way off, not here,
> Which is all right, and from what we hear
> The soldiers there only made trouble happen.
> Next year we shall be easier in our minds.

Next year we shall be living in a country
That brought its soldiers home for lack of money.
The statues will be standing in the same
Tree-muffled squares, and look nearly the same.
Our children will not know it's a different country.
All we can hope to leave them now is money.

In both Britain and the United States of America serious feeling and thought tend towards discontent with present apathy and rejection of one-sided solutions. We may now be ready to face the need to consolidate our Western political culture. This has become more and more feasible in the fields of economics, politics, defence and communications. Our whole culture can pull itself together, be united, and face its problems as a stronger and fresher entity. For, as even that frank critic of Western defects, Alexander Solzhenitsyn, has written, Western culture 'is so dynamic and so inventive that it will ride out even this impending crisis, will break up all its age-old misconceptions and in a few years set about the necessary reconstruction'. Let us hope so.

The United Kingdom—traditional champion and exemplar of that culture—has a history of playing a role in the world far greater than its mere military strength or physical size suggests. It has almost never been one of the two leading military powers, but it has relied on alliances, which have enabled it to defeat the great aggressors: Philip II, Louis XIV, Napoleon, William II of Germany, Hitler. But in spite of this reliance on the help of others the United Kingdom has usually been the soul of the resistance, and sometimes (as with both Napoleon and Hitler) the last remaining bastion, from which fresh alliances and counter-offensives could be organized. When William Pitt said 'England has saved herself by her exertions, and will, as I trust, save Europe by her example' he was expressing something of the spirit which might be expected to inform our attitude at all times.

In recent centuries Britain brought the principles of political civilization to half the world. The end of the empire has left us with an immense reserve of international knowledge and experience.

The people are ready for a lead, and they have a general

understanding of the issues. The British are stout-hearted, not to be overborne by threat or danger. And they know that they have something to defend:

> 'Dear-bought and clear, a thousand year,
> Our fathers' title runs.
> Make we likewise their sacrifice,
> Defrauding not our sons'.

Neither the energy nor the experience of the peoples of the United Kingdom is extinct. But it is true that at present they remain largely unharnessed and starved of leadership. Britain can yet give a lead as the finest and clearest-minded champion of the democratic culture. And a proper development of the alliances and other political arrangements of the West can serve as channels for her peoples' now latent powers.

Unfortunately, Britain has also a tradition of not standing firm, or seeing threats clearly until the danger is extreme and important positions have been lost. To some extent, this wasteful process can still be gone through without total disaster. But when it comes to the dangers of nuclear war, there is no leeway; it will either be prevented or not. Once started, it will no longer be a question of retreats, attrition, or 'losing every battle but the last' in the traditional manner.

For, I repeat, the perils of our situation are extreme. There is real danger of devastating nuclear attack, or of the destruction of our culture by a totalitarian terror regime, or both. In these circumstances it is hardly enough to suggest policies which are pretty reasonable for the price, and have a fair probability of success. It is essential that we should follow policies which give the greatest conceivable chance of survival. In particular, we must have policies which cannot be fatally misunderstood by our opponents.

If the techniques of war now seem capable of destroying our civilization, it is also true that sophisticated techniques of administration, transport and so forth are now capable of creating a united world. If the dangers are correctly handled, the rewards may be proportionately great. A programme for peace today must have a three-fold aim: first, it must prevent the destruction of the Western culture; second, it must work continually for the maintenance of a permanent truce between the two cultures, accepting for practical purposes the present existence of a divided world; and, third, it must hope for, wait for and encourage the emergence of the principle of civic consensus in the more backward despotic sphere, leading to the eventual establishment of a stable world peace.

We cannot afford policies which are not firmly based on a sound understanding of the main facts of the world situation. Anything else may result in the worst disasters we can imagine. On the other hand, if correct policies are followed, we have a real prospect of the gradual emergence of a truly peaceable world, and ever-increasing prosperity. Our grandchildren may be a handful of savages living in a radioactive desert, perhaps having passed some intervening years as serfs of a regressive tyranny; or they may be the free citizens of a happy and flourishing culture. It all depends upon the decisions we make now, and those decisions in their turn depend on a real effort of understanding. The dangers are extreme, the rewards enormous.

2

Soviet Motivations

Our relations with the Soviet Union are central to the whole refractory array of international problems before us, and therefore to the future of the world. So a deep and accurate understanding of the Soviet Union is crucial to our correct handling of these problems. The single error most likely to lead to trouble in the field of foreign affairs is misapprehension about the basic motives of the Soviet leaders. This applies both on the grand scale as we try to establish a peaceable and co-operative world, and more immediately as we handle the local crises which continually shake the international scene; that is, in both strategy and tactics.

For the crux of the international scene today is the relationship between different political cultures with alien histories, attitudes, and beliefs. As early as 1946, T. S. Eliot wrote in an extraordinarily perceptive essay introducing 'The Dark Side of the Moon':

We are, in fact, in a period of conflict between cultures—a conflict which finds the older cultures in a position of disadvantage: from lack of confidence in themselves, from divisions both internal and between each other, from the inheritance of old abuses from the past aggravated by abuses due to the hasty introduction of novelties. The liberal ... assumes ... that the cultural conflict is one which can, like political conflict, be adjusted by compromise, or, like the religious conflict, be resolved by tolerance ... The frantic attempt, either through assembling representatives of more and more nations in public, or through discussions between leaders of fewer and fewer nations in private, to find a political solution to what is not merely a political problem, can ... only lead to temporary and illusory benefits, unless the deeper problem is faced and pondered ...

7

In the modern world, moreover, developments in arms and communications have brought fundamentally divergent states and political cultures into extreme and sensitive contiguity. In his Nobel speech, Alexander Solzhenitsyn noted that in the old days disparate cultures were physically separated. Men were

> guided by their own experiences in their circumscribed localities, in their community, in their society, and lastly, on their national territory. Then it was still possible for a single pair of eyes to perceive and accept some common scale of values.

The differences between distant cultures were only known by report and to a few travellers; and they were so overt and extravagant at the most apparent level, that they did not invite any insular judgement. Padishah or Peacock Throne were instantly recognizable as alien: Secretary General or Trade Union Congress sound like the titles and institutions, with their associated attitudes, of the Western world. Nowadays, as Solzhenitsyn points out, mankind has been 'united', not in the old natural way into communities, but simply in a crude physical sense, with instant communication all over the planet of superficial information, while at the same time

> people in various places apply their own tried and tested scale of values to events, and insist self-confidently and stubbornly on judging only by their own scale.

The main source of difficulty and danger in world affairs today seems to be misunderstanding in Western minds of the nature of world politics, and in particular a sort of intellectual parochialism, combined with a lack of historical perspective, which leads people into failing to grasp the nature—and even the existence—of these profound differences between the essentially divergent political cultures which divide our planet. This results in attitudes to foreign affairs so fundamentally erroneous that they might easily lead to the destruction of our culture or even of the human race itself. We are all prone to parochial misconceptions about the deepest motivations underlying other political cultures. It requires a constant effort of intellect and imagination to free us from the habit of making such unconscious assumptions about the present thoughts and future actions of the Soviet leaders. Western policymakers have often failed to grasp these basic differences, which are not so much of opinion as of motivation. We see Political Man as a sort of android robot, programmed with one or another 'opinion'; if the opinion is removed and another substituted by demonstration and argument, his total behaviour will change. We think that we may thus 'rationalize' political conduct by applying criteria of reason and resonableness which seem natural to our own culture but are quite alien to others. In reality Political Man in different systems is not just the same creature holding different opinions, but rather a life-form which has evolved into radically different phyla, each with deep-rooted attitudes historically determined over long periods—and subject to natural selection as between different temperamental groups. In the USSR the present Marxist-Leninist ruling elements are actually unable to see the world in terms other than their own. Whatever else may be said about the Vietnam War, at least it is clear the the Politburo in Hanoi was simply not playing the game of escalations, signals and responses those in charge of operations against them thought reasonable and natural, and thus unreservedly applicable. It would be a pity to make the same sort of mistake on a global scale.

We may conveniently make a basic distinction between the 'civic' and the 'despotic' cultures. In the former, policy is articulated and decisions are made, in principle, in accordance with a balance of interests and views, through consultation with and acceptance by various sections of the community. In the 'despotic' culture decisions are made by a single man or group regarded as uniquely qualified, and the population is merely a passive element.

Not all despotisms had been expansionist. But Tsarism, as Marx noted, carried a tendency to universal expansion; while Communism was explicitly a world-idea, and Lenin and his successors ruled that only the Soviet model would serve. (Similarly, both traditions held the same view of the unofficial thinker; and Brezhnev's Russia resembles the Russia of Nicholas I far more closely than, for example, Britain resembles the Britain of 1830.) The despotic culture divides naturally into the two general types. In the traditional 'imperial' system it is assumed that the true form of the state has already been achieved; whereas the messianic revolutionary type seeks by an act of will to bring history to an eschatologically predetermined conclusion. The two varieties have much more in common with each other than they do with the Western culture. But above all, the present Soviet regime amounts to a fusion of the two.

In the Russian tradition, since Mongol times, the state had claimed absolute control over society as a matter of principle. The revolutionary counter-tradition which developed within it was equally total in outlook: the elect, with their perfect doctrine, would seize power with an absolute claim to rule over the population. Even before the Russian Revolution, Rosa Luxemburg had noted how the idea of the infallible Bolshevik Central Committee was no more than a mirror image of Tsarist autocracy, aggravated by the Leninists' 'Tartar-Mongolian savagery'. It is true that there has always been an alternative tradition in Russia, and that from about 1860 a Europeanized civic attitude had grown up, with courts, juries, eventually a fairly free press, and a Duma; but this development was crushed between the millstones of traditionalist and messianic despotism and the fruit of two generations of precarious civic development was destroyed. This may be seen as the main achievement of the October Revolution.

There have always been highly differing political cultures on the face of our planet. A periwigged Hanoverian king would never have thought that the intentions of a turbaned and scimitared sultan were the same as his own. Gladstone can hardly have believed the Mahdi's deepest motives to be much like those of a British Liberal. Nowadays the Politburo in Moscow wear Western suits and speak a variant of the Western political dialects. But the Soviet leaders are—as much as any Sultan or Madhi—the product of centuries of history very different from our own, and of a long-standing political psychology alien to ours in its motives, judgements and intentions.

Moreover, the messianic-revolutionary version of the despotic tradition believes itself, far more strongly than the older type, to be in possession of absolute political truth. Against it, no one has any rights. Leninism holds not only that all systems which deviate from the true belief are wrong, but also that conflict must go on, as a law of history, until they are destroyed. Every negotiation or discussion is part of a 'struggle'. The only question is, in Lenin's words, 'Who-whom?' In other words, who gains at whose expense? Leninism looks forward consciously to the imposition of the Leninist will throughout the world, far more explicitly than traditional Tsarist expansionism ever did.

The seizure of power in 1917 by a party which in 1912 had well under 10,000 members was followed by an intensive process through which, even within that narrow sect, a still narrower cadre survived to rule. After the destruction of all other segments of the political spectrum, the segment remaining was sliced thinner and thinner. Even within this narrow power group, by 1940 the situation was as if, in Britain, 90 per cent of Parliament, the Army officers, the economic elite, the journalists, the county, town and parish authorities, and the leaders of all organizations down to the Boy Scouts, had been eliminated. The Communists were already a radically different political species. Stalin's purge was a harsh form of unnatural selection which produced a yet more alien type.

The physicist Dr. Alexander Weissberg, a victim and student of the purge, notes of those who rose at the time, 'The choosing had been a very negative one. They were the men who had denounced others on innumerable occasions. They had bowed the knee whenever they had come up against higher authority. They were morally and intellectually crippled'. More than ever they were bearers of the doctrine 'Who-whom?' and of the absolute authority of the Party and its doctrine; and they came from precisely those strata which had never been touched by Westernization. Not only were Brezhnev, Suslov, Kosygin and others formed and selected by the purges; not only were many of the present leadership, (Brezhnev, Grishin, Gromyko, Kapitonov, Kosygin, Kutznetsov, Ponomarev, Suslov, Ustinov, Zimyanin) actually members of Stalin's own personally appointed Central Committee. It is also the unanimous view of all sections of unofficial thought in the USSR—Nadezhda Mandelstam, Academician Sakharov, Roy Medvedev—that the younger generation of *apparatchik*, the men now in their forties, are even more dogmatic and more dangerous in their total myopia about the doctrine and the system.

The leaders, then, and their subordinates and probable successors from the lower power-bases of the Party, are men whose attachment to the Leninist attitude is part of their whole personality, rather than a matter of the 'opinions' they hold, in the sense of accepting a view out of which they might be argued by logic or evidence. They were soaked in the despotic, and the despotic-revolutionary, tradition. They cannot see the world in terms other than those of their own history. First they have been determined by their whole background, and then specially selected for their suitability to the Leninist way of life. It is less a matter of 'ideology' than of an inability to think in any other categories. Brezhnev need not be envisaged as kneeling down and reciting the *Theses on Feuerbach* every night (any more than Richard Coeur de Lion spent much time reciting the Athanasian Creed). He has enough ideology to get along, and the rest is soaked into his bones.

This is not to say that conscious ideology does not play its part. We have accounts of long and serious sermons from Suslov, Ponomarev and others to representatives of foreign Communist Parties, even to the degree of insisting on a Marxist formulation that may be politically disadvantageous to the Party concerned. For example, the confidential Soviet advice to the Syrian Communist Party, published in the Beirut *Ar-Rayah* on 26 June 1972, and commented on at length by Mohammed Heikal in the Cairo *Al-Ahram* on 18 August 1972, can now certainly be accepted as genuine. It was a long, considered set-piece, in the preparation of which Soviet ideologists and political experts had made separate studies. It laid down Marxist criteria highly offensive to much of the Arab world: in particular asserting that 'there is no such thing as an Arab nation . . .'

> naturally the denial of the existence of the Arab nation is politically harmful, but to assert its existence in the programme [of the Syrian Communist Party] is not correct because Marxism-Leninism denies it.

Again, apart from the mere power-mania of the apparatus, the sole rationale of the disastrous collective farm system of agriculture is ideological. A few years ago, when a Politburo member suggested a sensible relaxation as the only way to the much-sought improvement in agricultural production, he (Voronov) was removed. Similarly with the general economic reforms which came up in the mid-sixties: either they have not been implemented, or they have been so modified as to deprive them of most of their benefits, for 'ideological' reasons.

The very acceptance of a closed ideology of absolute certainties provides the justification of rule, the mortar for the bricks of power and ambition. It is a further profound reason for their attitudes being so different from our own.

In insisting on the necessity of making a continual effort of the imagination and of the intellect, in order to avoid 'natural' misreadings of Soviet intentions, I am far from claiming that even careful Western students of the Soviet Union are immune from lapses. I remember once, when I was writing a book about the Stalin purges, discussing some of its military aspects with the late Tibor Szamuely (who had been brought up in Russia and followed a normal career for one of his generation, at Moscow University, in the Soviet Army, and in the Vorkuta labour camps). I said to him that I understood Stalin shooting Marshal Tukhachevsky, but I did not see why he shot Marshal Yegorov. Tibor, in his high Hungarian voice, instantly replied, '*Why not?*' This was, I realized at once, the answer. Though I had probably studied Stalin and Stalinism as intensely as any Westerner, and could hardly be accused of underestimating his ruthlessness, I still had not got right into his skin.

Stalin is not the whole of the Soviet Union and its history; but unthinking assumptions may still be made. As to Stalinism, the Westerner has a certain blockage against the real mental degradation of evil. My own book, *The Great Terror*, lacks at least one point which Solzehnitsyn gives us in *The Gulag Archipelago*. I do not attribute to the Secret Police anything in the way of decency or wisdom, but I do not quite show them as the bird-brained, sniggering torturers they really were.

I mention this to illustrate that an understanding of Soviet motives requires of all of us a continual effort to transcend the lazy application to them of our own deepset habits of thought. The important thing is not how much we approve or disapprove of the Soviet leaders but how much we understand them. One of the most simple and striking illustrations of the

Soviet attitude is perhaps to be found in their treatment of mere truth, mere fact, a point central to their whole attitude to the world. As Solzhenitsyn himself said (in his Nobel speech) nowadays, 'anyone who proclaims violence as his method is inexorably bound to choose the lie as his principle'.

Unacceptable events or persons from the past are simply not mentioned. At present there is no story, true or false, about the great purges of the 1930s which constitute the dominating event in producing the present Soviet Union, and many prominent Old Bolsheviks are virtually never mentioned at all.

This sort of thing is carried to the most extravagant lengths. When a new edition of the most used Russian dictionary came out in Khrushchev's time, it had a single detectable change from the previous one: *khrushch*, a type of beetle, had previously been described as 'deleterious to agriculture'. This phrase was now omitted. On the other hand at the time of Khrushchev's fall in 1964, a Soviet opera company was in Milan playing *Boris Godunov*. A new programme appeared, in which a minor character of that opera, 'Khrushchev', was transformed into merely 'a boyar'.

Soviet rewriting of encyclopedias constitutes another show-piece of the operation of the Soviet political mind. Many readers will have heard of the occasion when, after the fall of Beria, subscribers to the *Large Soviet Encylopedia* were sent a set of fresh pages on the Bering Sea and an obscure eighteenth century courtier called Bergholz, with instructions to remove certain unspecified, but numbered, pages with a razor blade and paste these in instead. When Malenkov lost the premiership, but not all his power, the next edition of the *Encylopedic Dictionary* differed from its predecessor solely in shortening his entry, making up space with a minor fortress, an engineer who had invented a six-wheeled bogie, and a hitherto neglected strawberry called *malengr*. An even more remarkable example came in the volume of the *Small Soviet Encyclopedia* which was rolling off the presses in June 1941. In some copies, evidently the earlier part of the print, Franklin Roosevelt appears as an agent of American business, and instigator of an imperialist war; in others, he has become a representative of the aspirations of the people and an opponent of fascist aggression.

The most vivid illustration of this attitude has, of course, been found in the manipulation of photographs. The most famous case is the classic picture of Lenin addressing a crowd, in which two other faces were previously visible by the rostrum: Trotsky and Kamenev. In the picture as it has appeared in Russia for the last forty years these have been eliminated. There are pictures of the delegates to party congresses, in which, for later versions, previously existing faces have been blurred into other people's greatcoats. There is too, a celebrated photograph of Stalin in exile with a handful of other revolutionaries; in the earlier version Kamenev is on his left, in the later he has become part of a tree.

The tradition continues in Brezhnev's USSR. In 1972, the Soviet authorities published a version of a photograph which, apparently, they did not realize they had already issued in 1971. Both versions were reprinted in the British magazine *Spaceflight*. They are absolutely identical except in one respect. They show the great genius of the Soviet space effort, Sergei Korolev —a former labour camp inmate who never concealed his contempt for the system, but whose name and role were kept from the world and the Soviet public until shortly before his death; the training director, Karpov, and four or five cosmonauts— Gagarin, Titov, Bykovsky, Popovich . . . and, now we come to the mystery. The later photograph has the above named only, the earlier has a further unknown figure who has disappeared in the 1972 one, being replaced by a piece of touched-up wall. We do not know why.

This alone constitutes evidence of a remarkable difference between our central attitudes and theirs. But if anyone still entertains the notion of a Soviet rationality similar to our own, let me recount a photographic tale which is stranger still. In the mid-1960s some of those shot after the notorious Bukharin trial in 1938 were rehabilitated—though a number were not, (which in itself is absurd, since the confessions of all linked them in a single close-knit conspiracy). The question now arose of rehabilitating Faizulla Khodzhayev, the Ubzek Communist leader who had been one of the victims. Meanwhile, a local Party history printed a photograph taken in the 1920s at the time of the seizure of power locally. As originally published, in those early days, it had shown Khodzhayev sitting in the front row. The officials of the Communist Party's Science and

Culture Department, and of *Glavit*, the censorship organ, were now faced with a ticklish problem. Khodzhayev had not yet been formally rehabilitated, but those in the Party machinery were plainly aware that the procedures were afoot. Thus, to blank him out altogether in favour of a potted palm would be political short-sightedness, while to put him in would be to anticipate official action impermissably. It is hard for us to imagine the debate that must have taken place at quite important levels; harder still to envisage the committee agreeing, when the solution was found, that this was a splendid idea. For the decision was to print the photograph with one small change —the concealment of the greater part of Khodzhayev's face behind a large beard which had not appeared in the original!*

I think most of us would agree that people who think like that are rather different from those we are used to.

It is the strangeness of the falsifications, the extravagant mania of the Party notion of the relation between power and truth, which make such details worth recounting. They may, one hopes, provide the sort of jolt necessary to see the Soviet leaders in their real, alien light. For these are not aberrations, but fair illustrations of the Soviet mind, of the attitudes of the Soviet political culture. It is that culture *as a whole* which is aberrant from our point of view.

Of course, all this photographic faking casts a particularly vivid light on the convoluted Soviet view of what is right and proper. More essential is the refusal to admit that crimes on an enormous scale have been committed. An entirely false account of the Katyn massacre is still maintained. Historic restitution is still denied to the victims of Kolyma. But as long as such things are suppressed, the present leaders remain not only the inheritors but also the accomplices of Stalinism—while continuing to maintain its principles on the issues of truth and tyranny.

Despotism—especially 'scientific', ideological despotism—

---

* The two versions are to be found in *K istorii Revolyutsii v Bukhare i natsional'nogo razmezhvaniya Srednei Azii*, by F. Khodzhayev, Tashkent 1932, and *Partiinaya Organizatsiya Tadzhikistana v 1924–1926 Godakh*, by A. V. Makashov, Dushambe, 1964. We chance to know from the literature that Khodzhayev never had a beard. (See Dr. Donald Carlisle in *Kritika* volume VIII, number 1, Fall 1971.)

which appears to be the rational, ordered form, in fact contains greater elements of irrationality than our own system. Ours, it is true, usually involves an attachment to ancient rights on a piecemeal and even sentimental basis not easily amenable to 'rationalization'. But it also contains the element of debate and argument, as well as a feeling for deeper and less conscious needs, even if these are not explicit. Despotism contains within itself all the elements of a more extreme irrationality—the elimination of real debate and criticism, and the idolization of premature political perfectionism. The backwardness of modern despotism resides not merely in its similarity to the bureaucratic empires of the past, but also in the factors thought to constitute its modernity. The millenarian promise that through the 'temporary' despotism of an elite of intellectual saviours the good society will be established on earth is an ancient fallacy, not a modern discovery. Marxism, with its claim to be 'scientific', is no such thing. The revelation of final answers in fields where none are available (the most unscientific of all procedures) uses the jargon of 'Science' in the nineteenth and twentieth centuries as it used those of 'Reason' in the eighteenth and 'Theology' in the sixteenth and seventeenth, as the most fashionable and convincing phraseology of the period.

Insofar as Marx tried to adopt scientific methods, by making empirical predictions against which his theories could be tested, he has long since proved wrong on every count. More important, the whole principle of the closed system has been devastated by Popper and others—so that, as Mr. Bryan Magee, the Labour MP, puts it, 'I do not see how any rational man can . . . still be a Marxist'. The irrationality at the core of Marxism has manifested itself revealingly in Marxist attachment to other pseudo-sciences, from Marx's own concern with phrenology to the various crackpot linguistic, aesthetic, medical and biological idiocies of the Communist epoch. The common factor is that these too offer quick and complete answers not otherwise available.

Soviet thought, indeed, is at a low level even within this context, through its reliance on persecution instead of argument. The closed ideology and lack of access to other thought, which have prevailed in the Soviet Union since its formation, led automatically to the progressive degeneration of the political mind, so that the present Soviet leaders are a group of rather bigoted fundamentalists. They are the product of a narrow system, and the main figures were moulded in the most soul-destroying and intellect-stunting period of Soviet rule, taking their first steps in the Stalinist apparatus during the great terror of the mid-thirties.

They are men, moreover, who no longer have the degree of detachment from a party machine previously thought necessary in all political leaders. They are now little more than ecto-plasm of that machine. This political system is gradually running down for want of any fresh energies, and is headed by men of little scope who are possessed of a dogmatic intolerance of all other forms of political life on this planet, and who dis-pose of an increasingly vast concentration of modern weapons. And they constitute the motive force—the only motive force—of Soviet foreign policy.

This view of the Soviet scene is shared by independent Soviet commentators like Andrei Amalrik, Soviet officials in private conversation, Western Communists with long-standing contacts in the Kremlin, leading Western journalists in Moscow of both left and right, and leading academic figures in the field of Soviet political studies. A typical diagnosis by Roger Garaudy when still a member of the Politburo of the French Communist Party was that

> the leaders who form the essential framework of the Party and the State were formed by Stalinism and put in position in Stalin's time on the basis of the criteria of the epoch: the acceptance of official dogmas, the fulfilment without discus-sion, at every level, of directives coming from above; and centralized, bureaucratic and authoritarian functioning.

As a result of this Garaudy, like Amalrik, saw no hope for the present leadership, nor need we be misled by their managing to be on their best behaviour on certain occasions. At their meeting with the Czechoslovak Communist leadership at Cierna-nad-Tisu, in the summer of 1968, though the discussions were sometimes fairly heated they remained 'comradely'. When, a few weeks later, the Czechoslovak leaders were arrested, subjected to physical violence, and paraded as prisoners before a jeering Soviet Politburo, they were quite unprepared for the change of tone. As one of the Czechs put it, while it was no surprise that the Russians were narrow-minded dogmatists, what came as a shock was to find that they were also 'vulgar thugs'. The low level of intrigue noted after that occasion, when they had to release the Dubcek's colleagues and return them to Prague, was equally striking—as when they promised, but failed to deliver to the plane until the others refused to go without him, their greatest bugbear, Kriegl, 'that damned Galician Jew', as Brezhnev put it.

The coarseness of the Stalinist tradition and its narrow-mindedness are faces of the same coin. The narrowness, the fundamentalist dogmatism, remains central to all pronouncements on the long-term ends of Soviet policy.

One of the most striking events to have taken place in the Soviet Union in recent years was on 22 February 1978, Soviet Army Day. As if to refute suggestions by Western well-wishers that the spirit of the regime has changed and that it regrets its Stalinist heritage, Dimitry Ustinov, Minister of Defence (and formerly Stalin's Minister of Armaments), addressed an audience of six thousand of the Soviet elite. He made two favourable references to Stalin, each time being interrupted by prolonged applause. The applause was, moreover, reported in *Pravda* the next day.

There could hardly have been a franker demonstration of the views and allegiances of those who rule the Soviet Union. Moreover, as the Soviet philosopher G. S. Pomerants remarked a few years ago, praise for Stalin when he was alive was not open and acknowledged praise for a system of lies and terror, since these were then denied and concealed; but now much of the truth has long been available in the USSR itself, so that (in Pomerants' words):

> to restore respect for Stalin, knowing what he did, is to establish something new, to establish respect for denunciations, torture, executions. Even Stalin did not try to do that. He preferred to play the hypocrite. To restore respect for Stalin is to set up a moral monstrosity by our banner . . . .

But Ustinov now makes it clear that destalinization, of which so much was once said, has not lasted, and to the degree that it happened at all has largely been made up for by re-stalinization, whose public principles have thus been so openly declared.

The present Soviet elite is not only the product of the frightful Stalinist selection process. Unlike some of the earlier Bolsheviks it also derives from precisely those archaic elements of society which were unaffected by the progressive 'Europeanization' of Russia in the last half century of Tsarist rule. Moreover, as Dr. Brzezinski has noted (*Newsweek*, 26 April 1971),

> We should not forget that the Soviet political leadership, composed of relatively simple men of strong ideological and nationalist motivations (a typical first post-peasant generation), is a classical example of the military-industrial complex; a very heavy proportion of the top Soviet leaders (by far more than in the US) are men with extensive personal backgrounds in the defence industries and in the armed forces. This is especially true of the Politburo and of the party Secretariat, and particularly of Brezhnev himself. Moreover, it is probably true that the Soviet military, traditionally excluded from the top policy councils are, as a group, more influential today than at any point since 1917.

The ruling group is thus (as Professor Pipes has said) not 'predisposed by its cultural background to regard itself as part of a broader international community' and has no conception of a stable world order.

There are people in the West who wish the Soviet leaders were friendly. They are uncomfortable when they hear proof to the contrary; and so they ignore it, cling to their delusions, try to shout it down. But I have yet to hear of anyone with a real claim to understanding the world today, and in particular the Soviet Union, who does not agree that the analysis given above is both true and vitally important.

The Soviet leaders are hostile in principle to all that we stand for. There is nothing secret about this. They state it quite openly in their public speeches in Moscow, in their world wide propaganda, in their indoctrination of their own populations. They attack us and our society continually. They build up vast armaments, and attack us for our lesser effort. They rule scores of subject peoples, and attack us as imperialists. Nor is this constant and virulent hostility difficult to understand. The average Briton has a perfectly clear mind on this subject. The question of how to abate or outface such hostility stands out as the central problem of foreign affairs.

Such are the facts. Are we to ignore them? Some people seem to think so. They think that peace is best served by pretending that all is well when it is not; by saying that the Soviet leaders are other than they are, and that their aims and practices are quite different from what we know them to be.

The record of delusion about the Soviet Union is bad enough, in all conscience. In the 1930s Stalin was able to deceive a wide range of Westerners about the fake Moscow trials, even such men as Sir Bernard Pares, one of the leading experts on Russia and Russian history, and also Julian Huxley, Harold Laski and the Webbs. We can do without a repetition.

The principles of Soviet policy, both at home and abroad, have been in effect to deny the right of existence to non-communist (or deviant communist) ideas or regimes. *And this has never been concealed.* Major ideological analysis by or on behalf of the Party leadership has always clearly asserted these principles. It is of course true that there has been an accompanying smoke-screen of more 'liberal', tolerant and peaceable remarks by various sponsors of Soviet propaganda in the West. But (as Professor Hugh Seton-Watson has said) it seems a mistake to believe that

> What 200,000 Communist party officials, from Brezhnev down to the secretaries of party branches in factories or collective farms, tell their subjects is all camouflage: The *real* views of the Soviet leaders are what some nice guy from the Soviet delegation at the UN said over a quiet drink, or what an itinerant midwestern scientist heard from some friendly academician in Novosibirsk.

We should do the Communist Party of the Soviet Union the justice of accepting that it believes what it says. The Soviet leaders really seek a world dominated by their system. They are really, in the long run, not prepared to accept a continuance of the Western and democratic order. It is only at a much lower level, that of deceptive propaganda, that any question arises of an end to this central intransigence.

This is a clear and understandable position. It is compatible with wishing to avoid nuclear war, and seeking a certain style of detente. But it is, all the same, one of a central and basic hostility to other forms of political life.

And what are the prospects of improvement? Barring some unforeseen internal collapse—which reputable observers like M. Michel Tatu of *Le Monde* regard as possible—one does not envisage any rapid evolution to normality under the present rulers, or their successors. Political cultures evolve slowly. Nor need instant democracy be an automatic success; as Solzhenitsyn points out, Russia's brief experience of this in 1917, when it was unprepared for it, had to be paid for by sixty years of unexampled despotism. He looks back to an autocracy which was not perfect but at least allowed genuine progress, and permitted large areas of legality and of free expression—the Russia of the post-Emancipation period. In those days a properly organized legal system came into being, and juries actually acquitted enemies of the State. This is not the place to rehearse the history of Russia between 1860 and 1917; but at least it will not be denied that some elements of liberty and of civic order existed, and that there was a hope and a good possibility of their evolving into a broader and more democratic system.

Solzhenitsyn, like all non-schematic students of peoples and their history, understands that Russia has her own traditions. He sees the roots of a specifically Russian democracy not only in the promise of its immediate prerevolutionary years, but also in old Novgorod; in the pre-Petrine Assemblies; in the village mirs; in the Cossack Republic at Zaporozhe. And it is clear that he does not expect an evolution precisely similar to that of any of the Western countries. As he notes in his Letter to the Patriarch, the past fifty years have been wasted, and more than wasted, in Russia. 'Half a century of the past has already been lost, and I am not talking about trying to save the present. But how are we to save the future of our country?'

The greater part of the slow progress made after the 1860s has been lost. If a start could be made by simply eliminating the extremes of totalitarianism, by initiating and planting areas of legality, that would indeed be a real beginning. Academician Sakharov is often presented as one who sees more hope in immediate democratization. But he too speaks of the 'many fine democratic steps beginning with the reforms of Alexander the Second', and admits that the present vicious circle 'cannot be overcome in a short time'.

From the point of view of the West it is true that, as Engels commented of an earlier time,

> As soon as Russia has an internal development, and with that, internal party struggles, the attainment of a constitutional form under which these party struggles may be fought without violent convulsions . . . the traditional Russian policy of conquest is a thing of the past!*

That has not yet come. In the meantime, various evolutions and revolutions are possible. But for the immediate future Russia is ruled by oligarchs who are faced by a society tending in every respect away from their concepts, but who possess an immensely powerful instrument for blocking social and political change. In foreign affairs, we have the unpleasant problem of an inept Soviet leadership with huge military resources, answerable to none, and possessed of a surly hostility to all other forms of political life.

On the other hand the Soviet interpretation of world affairs does not in principle allow of dangerous initiatives. They believe that the laws of history are on the Soviet side and although Marxism insists on continual pressure to keep things going in the right direction, it does not countenance initiatives which might bring unnecessary risk. This may give us time.

One should not deny in principle that a communist party in power can evolve towards the Western 'civic' political system. The examples of Czechoslovakia and, earlier, Hungary, show that this is now possible. In Hungary the Communist Party virtually collapsed, but the Czechoslovakian case was a genuine evolution. The question, an evidential rather than a conceptual one, is whether there are any potential forces within the CPSU to match the Goldstückers and Siks and Dubceks of Czechoslovakia. I know of no student of politics who would give any answer except a resounding 'no'. The Soviet *apparat* is not

---

* From Engel's essay "The Foreign Policy of Russian Czardom".

comparable to those of the satellite states. It does not consist of men who joined the Party before it came to power and then found that their political conceptions were not fulfilled. It does not contain the rehabilitated remnants of opposition movements, their minds—in some cases—wonderfully cleared by the experience of prison and torture. On the contrary, in Moscow we find at the upper level the traditional Stalinist cadre, the selected few whose moral and intellectual qualities enabled them to pass through the blood-bath of 1937–1938 unharmed; and the process of selection, stretching over fifty years, has produced a very definite human type.

It has also produced a very solidly established, traditional-minded interest-group, a large number of hard-bitten operatives constituting both a tightly organized machine, and at the same time a social caste deeply imbued and indoctrinated with a system of ideas; or rather, a whole psychological 'set', centering on the notion (as in similar groups in history), of their divine right to rule Russia.

Perhaps there are exceptions, men who in spite of the rigours of their political upbringing are capable of wider judgement. How any such individuals could influence matters is not apparent. It may be said that in a sense Khrushchev filled this role: but as Pietro Nenni pointed out after his fall, he was unable to overcome the system, in spite of his ascendancy. *I* would add that though he plainly saw that something was wrong, he never really escaped from his conditioning.

All the same, the Khrushchev experience may possibly indicate the only chance there is of a Russia, while still under the control of the CPSU, yet evolving towards freedom. In Russian history, the great reforms have usually been carried out by despotic rulers overcoming the objections of their own ruling classes. This applies, of course, to Peter the Great and to Alexander II and the liberation of the serfs. To a limited and inadequate degree, the comparable measures of the Stolypin period might perhaps have modernized Russia, given a longer period. The rise of a new despot to the top in the Kremlin might—I only say might—mark a similar change. But it might not. There have been plenty of non-reforming despots in Russia. Furthermore, in the current state of the Party there seems little prospect of anyone trying (as Khrushchev failed), to establish that total control over the Party which Stalin had. When one thinks of the long, difficult, cunning and ruthless campaign by which Stalin established his supremacy, it seems unlikely that it could be repeated. Apart from anything else, his colleagues and rivals could never quite believe the truth about his machinations. The present generation know the possibility perfectly well and would almost certainly be able to detect and thwart such moves. Moreover, in the fourteen years since the fall of Khrushchev, all the tendencies towards even moderate change which manifested themselves before have been weakened and then abandoned in every field. The Party had an opportunity and decisively rejected it.

Perhaps the most realistic attitude for the West, barring total and unforseeeable change in the Kremlin, is to understand the dangers and revert to a sensible policy of unprovocatively matching the USSR in armament, and blocking Society expansionism. This would, however intransigent their ideological mood, divert them into a period of watching and waiting for an opportunity—as happened after the defeat in Poland in 1920, until 1939. Such a 'temporary' suspension of expansionism would allow the positive forces in the USSR time to develop: even perhaps produce an evolution towards sanity, a gradual crumbling of the ideological foundations in the ruling group itself.

If the regime survives, hopes of peace would centre on such a limited evolution towards the progressive abandonment of its total claims in the world. This can best be attained by denying the Kremlin the possibility of achieving these aims and at the same time making clear the advantages to be gained by co-operation rather than conflict.

Policies now being pursued by the West seem dangerously close to the exact opposite: allowing excessive Soviet arms and expanionism, while giving them trade and other advantages as a reward for hostility rather than friendship.

The military strength, and the political determination, of the Soviet Union are clear enough. Equally relevant to considerations of sound foreign policy are the many weaknesses of their system. The USSR now leads only in one area—the military. It has an overwhelming armament, especially in Europe, and it faces opponents who are reluctant to match it in this field.

Otherwise, the USSR has, quite simply, lost the race in every sense. Its economic system slips further and further; even its gross national product is being overtaken by Japan and is about to be overtaken by West Germany, leaving Russia around the same comparative level as in 1914.

It is a system which no longer inspires, hardly even interests, opinion in the outside world; it has run out of ideas and finds apathy among its masses (tempered by riots), and hostility from its intelligentsia.

Like an underdeveloped country its exports are mainly raw materials and its imports technological products. It relies on the West to save it from the consequences of its disastrous agricultural policy, and for as much advanced technology as it can assimilate.

To gain some idea of the extent of the transformation in agriculture, for instance, it is useful to remember that before the First World War Russia was by far the most important grain exporting country in the world. Her grain exports were more than double those of the USA and constituted nearly one-third of the total world grain market. Today Russia seems well on the way to becoming one of the world's leading importers.

Figures published by the Food and Agriculture Organisation in 1970, after recent 'reforms' were having their greatest effects, showed that one American working on the land fed himself and thirty-nine others on a high protein diet, while one Soviet citizen working on the land fed himself and six others, on a largely starchy diet. As to productivity, even in the field of grain the USSR uses eight times as many workers as the USA to produce from thirty per cent more arable land less than ninety per cent of US grain for a population twenty per cent larger.

The system, far from tending to rationality, places a premium on quick and spectacular results however obtained. A. N. Larionov, First Secretary of the important Ryazan Province and a full member of the Central Committee for many years, sought esteem in Khrushchev's time by promising to double his province's meat production in a year. He succeeded in this, with the support of all his subordinates, by slaughtering all the milk cows and breeding stock, and illegally buying cattle on a large scale in other provinces (with funds illegally diverted from the purchase of machinery) and so on. After a brief triumph and promises of even better next year, Larionov, now a Hero of Socialist Labour and holder of the Order of Lenin, had to commit suicide in 1960 when it came out that he had ruined the area; his many imitators in other provinces disappeared. This is a spectacular example, but one which is typical of a whole range of continuing scandals and debacles at every level.

It is an extraordinary fact that the USSR ranks very low in almost all economic fields in comparison even with the other countries of the Soviet bloc. It is lowest in the rate of increase in production, lowest in standard of living, lowest in the use of fertilizers, lowest in grain productivity per acre and even runs fourth (after East Germany, Czechoslovakia and Poland) in gross national product per head.

These weaknesses should strengthen the hope that the Western allies may be able to convince the Soviet leaders that a forward policy cannot be sustained. Some Westerners speak as though failure to reach an arms agreement would result in an arms race in which the Soviet leaders could pour limitless new resources into weaponry. On the contrary, the Soviet economy is grossly overstrained in keeping up its present armament.

The concentration of all the efficient elements of the economy into war production has created an armament of unrivalled power. It is true that any given weapon system costs far more effort than in the West, owing to the inbuilt deficiencies of the system, but the sheer amount of investment in arms more than compensates, so far, for this defect, while the rest of the economy is milked of its most productive elements. Owing to 'security' considerations, there is even virtually no 'spin-off', as occurs in the West, from defense into the general economy. And the technological gap between the USSR and the West widens continually.

Yet, it will be said, the Soviet Union is equipped with an impressive array of modern weaponry, mostly developed at home. And this is perfectly true, just as it is true that the USSR produced an effective fusion bomb and orbited a satellite before the United States did. The point is that in all these cases the essential principles were already established, and the problem was, strictly speaking, one of an engineering rather

than of basic scientific research or discovery. As a result the
USSR is technically ahead in a number of important military
fields not because of any superiority in research, but because the
West, though fully capable, has not proceeded with development—a political rather than a technological weakness. The
sheer effort that goes into Soviet research and development is
far greater than in the West; and though a much higher proportion of it is wasted, there is enough to give a margin. In *basic*
research, however, the West is always ahead, and any Soviet
superiority can only be achieved when no important new
developments are required. This explains the uproar over the
cruise missile and the neutron bomb, infuriating proof that the
USA is technically a generation ahead.

The only way the USSR make up for this deficiency is by
establishing a parasitical relationship with Western technology,
milking it as an ant does an aphid.

The continued Soviet backwardness in technology always
surprises people who know that there are research scientists in
the USSR well up to the highest Western standards, and, there
have been good scientists in Russia since Lomonossov in the
eighteenth century. Part of the answer may be found when we
consider that there was a high standard of science in the ancient
world which was also not translated into technology. The
reasons seem to be similar, and to be of a social and political
nature—the reliance of the social order on a huge, but unpaid or
ill-paid working force. More generally, Soviet culture is not of
its very nature easily able to generate technological progress;
this has always been the mark of the open society alone.

The Soviet class or caste system inherent in these arrangements has comparable social defects. In Russia these inequalities
are not only due to differences in income, as in the West, but
include inequalities founded on law or custom, as in feudal
times: the 'special shops' for the privilegentsia where rare goods
can be obtained at particularly easy prices, the fact that an
apparatchik can visit the West at the state's expense, but a
worker cannot go there at all. About one third of all Communist
Party members hold down the highest paid economic jobs, and
Soviet income tax is far easier on higher incomes than is our
own. This new class is more unpopular with the second-class
citizens who constitute the mass of the population than is any

bourgeoisie in the West. Mass resentment is never far from the surface.

When the last time that the police have fired on strikers in Britain or America? In Russia and Poland the answer is, in the 1970s. What other great nation has seen, time and time again, important provincial cities taken over by spontaneous workers' strikers and uprisings? What has happened in the past ten or fifteen years in towns from Chimkent to Dnepropetrovsk has not been sufficiently understood here. The equivalent in Britain would be food-riots in Middlesborough, with dozens shot dead by police and army; strikes, developing into demonstrations in Aberdeen, with hundreds of casualties, nationalist demonstrations in Merthyr Tydfil, scores shot, hundreds arrested . . . and so on, in dozens of incidents. Such facts (though not repelling prominent members of Labour's National Executive Committee) might well distress workers in the West who had been made aware of them. More important, they indicate a basic weakness, even a philosophical error, in the position of the Soviet leadership.

Again, the mutiny on the Soviet warship *Storozhevoy* in November 1975 was reported in the West, but without much comment. Imagine if such a mutiny, and attempt to take the vessel into a neutral port, had taken place in the British or American Navies. What an outcry about symptoms of a collapse of morale would have been heard! And rightly. Nothing really comparable has taken place since the mutiny on the battleship *Potemkin* in 1905, which presaged the downfall of the then Russian state.

One shrewd analyst, Professor Richard Pipes, adds a further general point:

Even more significant, however, is the fact that the people of the Soviet Union are utterly exhausted. The country had been mobilized in 1914 and except for brief respites has not been allowed since then to return to normal life. Their fatigue is so profound that neither exhortations nor alarms can shake them from it. They require three things of which they have been deprived for the past half a century; peace, privacy, and prosperity, probably in that order.

The position of the independent thinker or writer in the USSR is well known, and needs no elaboration here. It must be unique in history that so large a section of the creative minds of a country are in exile—that emigre literature now ranks far higher than that written at home.

Exile is not the ideal place for a writer. However, the advantages can be seen from some actuarial facts which are of remarkable interest. With all there is to be urged in favour of a writer remaining in his home country, it is nevertheless the case that many of Russia's leading writers went into exile in 1917— the earlier Nobel Prize winner Ivan Bunin, for example. Some of them, like Bunin himself, continued to write. Almost all lived a good deal longer than those who remained. A glance through the contents page of the *Penguin Book of Russian Verse* (1962) shows that in the post-revolutionary period the average life-span of those noted as dying in exile is just over 72; and of those dying in the USSR just over 45! And those who were not killed had little cause to enjoy life; they include Pasternak and Akhmatova, of whose troubles the world is aware, be sidessuch men as Zabolotsky who survived labour camp to be rehabilitated alive. In addition to the five known executions or deaths in camp there were three suicides.

To summarise: a condition of sharp hostility has existed between the Soviet state and the best minds in the country from the start, and still persists, as part of the whole ideological system. Among workers, intelligentsia, peasants, minorities, the regime has lost credibility. It has nothing interesting to say to any but its privileged class. Otherwise, it can rely on inertia of mind, on the persistence of old phrases and fables among the usual supporters of the established order anywhere—the ignorant, the indoctrinated, and the chauvinistic.

All the pressures are towards an evolution. The economic, social, ethnic, intellectual forces all tend to thrust the Soviet government into directions more suitable to the needs of its own population and the necessities of world peace. These forces are opposed by the dead hand of ideology, of Party interest, of general inertia. More than any regime in the past, communist rule in the USSR is based on the construction of a political machine capable of containing and outfacing the natural tendencies of its subjects.

Unfortunately, none of this affects the fact that the regime has built up its present enormous armed forces, and entered into a policy of advance on the world front. The result, indeed, has been such that at Party Congresses Brezhnev's main reports have lately consisted largely of critical (and implicitly pessimistic) accounts of developments at home, balanced by well-founded boasts about the armed forces and foreign policy.

The weaknesses at home nevertheless imply a point beyond which the USSR could not match the West in armaments, simply from over-strain of the economic base. There can be no need for panic about a limitless arms race. Once the West committed itself to reasonable strategic and conventional parity, and to firm diplomatic action, the USSR would have little choice—whatever its longer term intentions—but to accept the situation.

More generally, though the propects of an early evolution of the Soviet regime into a cooperative and peaceable member of the world community are low, there is a greater likelihood of an economic and technological decline, to the degree that the USSR may hardly rank as an advanced country in a decade or so. This does not affect the urgency of the present world crisis. But it does offer us the hope that, if we handle it correctly, it may gradually become less dangerous.

3

Detente?

'Detente' is a pleasant-sounding general word, giving an impression of good will, optimism, and increasing amicability among the states subscribing to it. It may seem cruel to submit this heartwarming word to a closer analysis, and in particular to draw attention to the interpretation placed on it by others, notably the USSR. For the West tends to think that the frequent recitation of this brief and easily mastered spell will make all well on the international scene.

Gromyko, who is in charge of foreign operations, has formulated the principles of Soviet foreign policy in the era of detente in terms of the utmost clarity, and his words alone should suffice to prevent any misunderstanding:

> The Communist Party subordinates all its theoretical and practical activity in the sphere of international relations to the task of strengthening the positions of socialism, and the interests of further developing and deepening the world revolutionary process. *The Foreign Policy of the Soviet Union,* Moscow (1975).

In other words nothing must stop Soviet support for 'proletarian' (i.e. Communist) movements in the West and 'national liberation' (i.e. Communist-sponsored) movements in the Third World. This proposition has been continually asserted—as by Brezhnev at the 25th Party Congress. It has the corollary that 'detente' is not to be interpreted as in any way hampering the progress of Soviet-aided attempts to destroy the pro-Western position anywhere in the world. 'Detente' indeed is defined in Soviet statements as a 'method of struggle'. And in practice it has not excluded the sight of Soviet tanks rumbling into Saigon and Luanda, and nearly into Tel Aviv.

A usual formulation is that, like the 'class struggle', the 'ideological struggle' between the Communists and ourselves must continue as strongly as ever. Just as 'class struggle' on the world stage does not mean supporting the aims of genuine proletariats but merely of any political forces whatever which serve Soviet interests, so 'ideological struggle' does not mean— as some Westerners seem to think—a harmless campaign of honest argument in which the best man wins. On the contrary, its main components are: (a) an increase in anti-Western propaganda by pro-Soviet groupings in the West and Soviet radio broadcasts; (b) an intensification of anti-Western 'vigilance' and militarist propaganda in the USSR; (c) the suppression of pro-Western (and indeed pro-Maoist, pro-Islamic and other anti-Soviet) voices wherever possible; (d) a soft-spoken, weasel-word 'dialogue' with any Western elements —Christian, trade union, or whatever—who may have failed to notice (a), (b), and (c) and in spite of everything still present passive targets to the surprised and delighted Marxist-Leninist. Thus for the Kremlin, detente is simply a matter of verbal tactics comparable to those adopted by the Sun in Aesop's fable, when the Wind's attempt to make the Traveller shed his coat by violent blasts has failed, and the tactic of friendly warmth proves more successful.

Brezhnev has stated the political results he seeks from detente in the Western capitals clearly enough.

> In conditions of international tensions, in bourgeois countries, the reactionary elements become active, the military raise their heads, anti-democratic tendencies and anti-Communism are strengthened. And conversely, the past few years have shown quite clearly that, in conditions of slackened international tension, the pointer of the political barometer moves left.*

Translated out of Sovietese this signifies that 'detente' is pursued with the aim of weakening Western vigilance and making it easier for appeasers and pro-Soviet elements to come to power.

* Speech to the Conference of European Communist Parties at Karlovy Vary, April 24, 1967.

It is important indeed that 'detente' is not interpreted as granting the West equivalent rights. The 'ideological struggle' is to be conducted by freely operating Communist Parties and presses in Western Europe and the United States, but by the total suppression of Western-oriented ideas in the Communist bloc. The CPSU Party Secretaries who are in charge of ideology and relations with foreign countries, particularly Boris Ponomarev and Mikhail Suslov, attend the Congresses of Communist Parties in the West, making speeches and giving general guidance or advice to them in their struggle for power. There are no legal parties representing Western views in the Communist bloc, of course, but it would be regarded as quite unacceptable for a Western Socialist statesman to attend a congress of Hungarian or Polish Social Democrats in exile, or underground within the countries concerned.

According to Soviet theory detente is compatible with expansionism, and Soviet practice has provided a series of examples. But how was it possible for such actions as the Soviet-Cuban offensive in Africa to continue for so long before it was noted that this made nonsense of friendly agreement on armaments or anything else? And even, in many Western cases, not to have been noted yet?

The idea that we should simply permit these adventures is sometimes supported by the argument that African states should not 'be forced to choose' between the Soviet and Western side. But, as John Stuart Mill wrote,

> The doctrine of non-intervention, to be a legitimate principle of morality, must be accepted by all governments. The despots must consent to be bound by it as well as the free states. Unless they do, the profession of it by free countries comes but to this miserable issue, that the wrong side may help the wrong, but the right must not help the right. Intervention to enforce non-intervention is always rightful, always moral, if not always prudent.

Failure to react has produced ever-increasing pressure, as the Soviet movement gathers momentum, for them to capitalize on the lack of Western resistance. The Kosygin-Brezhnev team has been considerably bolder than Khrushchev was in his closing phase. The decision to provide massive military aid to

North Vietnam followed Khrushchev's overthrow. The Soviet naval presence in the Indian Ocean began in 1967 and was fully deployed only in 1968. Moreover, the decision to accelerate the construction of Soviet inter-continental ballistic missiles was taken by Khrushchev's successors.

We are told that if the Western powers make things difficult for Brezhnev and his colleagues by not accepting detente on Soviet terms, the present leadership will be overthrown by a dangerous and powerful 'hard-line' faction. This has been a perennial theme in the West on every occasion when the USSR has sought an agreement, since the time in the late 1940s when Edward Stettinius was assuring the President of the United States that Stalin was in danger of being overthrown by 'extremists' for his efforts to achieve a settlement. Moreover, even if the 'hard-liner' danger were as stated, we should not accept the supposed conclusion and settle at once on Brezhnev's terms. For that would be like saying, 'If you do not let this chap cut your throat now he has asked so politely, ruder fellows will come along and absolutely insist on it'.

None of this is, of course, to deny the possibility of faction in the Politburo. And it is conceivable that if Brezhnev fails in his attempt to get something for nothing, his rivals might overthrow him and revert to other tactics, or, indeed, that he himself might do so. But the existence or otherwise of a supposedly powerful, organized group of anti-Brezhnevites should not determine our own tactics. For we know that Brezhnev too is seeking military and political advantage rather than any profound long-term improvement in the Soviet relationship with the West.

As to the scope of Soviet ambitions, in June 1968 Foreign Minister Gromyko flatly asserted in his speech to the Supreme Soviet:

> The Soviet Union is a great power situated on two continents, Europe and Asia, but the range of our country's international interests is not determined by its geographical position alone . . . the Soviet people do not plead with anybody to be allowed to have their say in the solution of any question involving the maintenance of international peace, concerning the freedom and independence of the people and our country's extensive interests. This is our right, due to the Soviet Union's position

as a great power. During any acute situation, however far away it appears from our country. the Soviet Union's reaction is to be expected in all capitals of the world.

One would have thought this claim to a place in the sun was unequivocal. Yet even here some Westerners have been found to extract a fairly harmless intent from it. They argue that all Gromyko said, and so all the Soviet Union wants, is the status of a global power co-equal with the United States. On this argument, the Soviet Union has for decades put in an enormous effort and over-strained its economy for the right to have its opinion 'listened to' in discussions of world problems. What nonsense! And if we interpret it as meaning that the Kremlin simply wants a half-share with the West in every sphere, it is still nonsense! Are we really to envisage a peaceable world in which every country is ruled by a stable coalition of communists and democrats? Or alternate countries are communist and non-communist, with no attempt to spread the power of the former into the latter? The idea falls down on grounds of common-sense, apart from the well-known and publicly proclaimed motivations of the Soviet leadership towards the triumph of their system throughout the world.

It is true that the Kremlin makes mistakes. I was once asked by an American Senator, while discussing mistakes made by the West, whether the Russians did not make them too. I said he could check this by simply looking out along Washington's Mall. If it had been a matter of our mistakes alone, KGB troops would have been marching along it that very day . . .

It is sometimes argued that Soviet expansionism is not always successful; since they have, for example, been expelled from Egypt and Somalia, therefore they will be expelled from Angola and elsewhere. The logical fallacy is obvious enough, but the whole point is worth considering as an instance of comfortable delusion.

The particular circumstances of Soviet expulsion from a country often takes us to the heart of the motivations behind Soviet foreign policy. In Egypt, for example, while their alliance with Sadat was at its closest, they were simultaneously mounting a plot to replace him with their own man, and when the plot was discovered they naturally lost credit with the Egyptian government. But this has always been Soviet practice: in 1927 their alliance with Chiang Kai-shek was accompanied by quite obvious political moves to undermine him, which naturally ensured his hostility.

Yet the logic is unassailable. An ally can never be entirely reliable, since his interests may differ sooner or later from those of the USSR; so it makes sense to replace him by someone more amenable. Naturally, this does not always work. But it would be facile optimism to think that one can merely say, 'Let the Soviets occupy any country they like; the local nationalists will soon get tired of them'. The example of Egypt can be countered, for the present at least, by that of South Yemen; while Cuba remains a devoted client state. It is also clear that there is a difference between a country which is physically able to expel Soviet 'advisers', and one like Angola where an attempted coup has actually been put down by Cuban mercenaries.

At best, such attitudes imply that one should not worry about Russian control of, or close alliance with, Third World countries, on the grounds that it may be temporary; but even such temporary control or presence might be extremely damaging to the Western interest. The Soviet base at Berbera no longer exists; but for some years it gave the Russians greatly increased leverage in the Indian Ocean, which might have proved highly damaging if a major crisis had arisen. Benign neglect of Soviet moves in such areas is indistinguishable from the old notion, so beneficial to aggressors, that this or that particular bit of territory is not vital to us—'Mourir pour Danzig?'

Of course, the loss of any particular African or Asian territory is not in itself the end of the democratic world. But how many have to go before we are entitled to feel a little anxious? There is already a tendency to think of only Western Europe, North America, the Japan-Australia area and perhaps Israel, as warranting serious defence. Yet if the USSR were to gain effective control of all 'expendable' parts of Asia and Africa the reward in raw materials alone would be enormous, to say nothing of strategic advantages. So, the struggle against Soviet penetration of these areas must continue, and we must ignore the notion, at least locally, no fundamental differences exist between ourselves and the USSR; this is a parochial delusion.

Acceptance of this double standard by Westerners is part of a more general failure of nerve. There are few Western countries which now publicly rebuff and refute the verbal aggressions of the Communist states, as the first post-war Labour Government and its contemporaries in the West did.

The policies which have come to be known as 'detente' were not originally envisaged in terms of unilateral surrender. While agreement was to be sought in various fields, with a general moderating of international bitterness, it was widely thought that any Soviet departures from these principles should be met by a firm attitude on the part of the Western powers. If (as many of us believe) the concept of detente was based on a misunderstanding of the nature and depth of Soviet motivations, it seems true that it also involved a misunderstanding of Western politics. Political action by the West depends very much on the degree of public support at home. Over a period of years the public was told that the Russians were no longer to be regarded as enemies, but rather as prospective partners in an amicable world community, and then suddenly, during the Angola crisis, it was asked to support firm action; naturally the public was confused, unprepared. It is an essential fallacy of 'detente' that one can continually assure the public that the Russians are amicable peace-seekers, while also trying to maintain a firm attitude towards them when they lapse from the role we have given them. In the US the Congress-media establishment was incapable of rousing itself from its deep dream of peace at short notice. Kissinger blamed them; logically he was right, but his entire policy had contributed to that mood.

This surrender includes a reluctance to deal with or denounce active Soviet subversion of the rest of the world, let alone to match it. Let us imagine that during troubles in, say, Albania, the French Foreign Legion goes in and brings a pro-Western group to power. The President of the United States makes continual speeches to the effect that Communism will not be tolerated in the West, but Western ideas must be freely admitted to Communist countries. His representatives at the highest level attend meetings, not of 'dissidents', but of groups openly working for the overthrow of the Soviet system; they

bring the official greetings of the Western leaders, with encouragement to continue until the political and social order is
destroyed. Huge American naval manoeuvres take place in
the seas off the Soviet White Sea, Black Sea and Pacific coasts.
Meanwhile, after Italy has attempted to change sides, an anti-
Communist regime is installed there by American arms . . .
What is wrong with this picture? It is, of course, the dramatiza-
tion of a mirror image of what the Russians have done and are
still doing. Naturally, I do not recommend that the West follow
the Soviet example in every particular. But it should at least be
ready to stand firm against Soviet expansionism, and state its
own case firmly in all the international arenas.

In the West, detente is not seen as a 'method of struggle'. It
is seen as a method of peaceful agreement. The two opposed
concepts have resulted in a costly asymmetry. The need for a
fair and symmetrical balance between the West and the Soviet
Union is quite simply met: we should accept the Soviet definition
of detente as a form of struggle and not of friendship, which excludes any departure from 'ideological warfare', or the granting
of a unilateral right of intervention in Africa or elsewhere. If and
when we can induce them to agree to something less bleak, so
much the better—and it is certainly up to us to seek ways of
doing so, since they plainly will not. But until that happy day, we
should match them in these fields as much as in armaments.

It is sometimes urged that goodwill and mutual tolerance, a
'mellowing' of the Soviet system, are gradually being achieved
as by-products of piecemeal trade, cultural, diplomatic, and
other bonds—somewhat as the Lilliputians sought to bind
Gulliver with a thousand weak threads, each strengthening the
last. In this way, it is hoped to avoid direct confrontation even
on the human rights issue, since *apparatchik* resistance will
eventually be outflanked in a painless manner.

It is true that cultural exchanges have some minimal effect in
eroding the rigour of monopolistic party conviction in a limited
circle of Soviet citizens; and even make a small contribution to
the easier movement of people. The Kremlin has made this
small concession under carefully controlled conditions, partly
motivated by the need for scientific progress. If it does produce
a certain increased alienation in some intellectuals, that
alienation is already present in the USSR, and the whole raison

d'être of the dictatorship is the containment and suppression of the alienated. The state and party machine built by Stalin and his successors is designed for that purpose. The central problem before us is to ensure that the state and party, rather than suspect subjects, develop a tolerance of the outside world. Naturally, in the long run, we must rely on social and intellectual pressures within the USSR to secure the evolution or elimination of the regime; but, as dissidents so often tell us, these pressures are impotent without active Western encouragement and support.

Discussions among American academics about the extent to which Soviet society may be opened up by the contacts formed through detente are often more sanguine than seems justified. They now visit academic institutions and have other contacts in the USSR, when formerly they had virtually none, so they generalize from a few personal experiences. It is noticeable that these views are not shared by Western journalists in Moscow, although they too have increased their contacts in recent years.

For even these academic contacts are not so impressive: over a period of twenty years a few thousand academic visitors came from all the Western countries taken together, and most of these were on very brief visits. In the seventeen years up to 1976 fewer than 300 scholars from all the Western countries had taught in Soviet institutions for a term or more, and since then the figures seem to have risen only slightly. When we consider (as Professor Robert F. Byrnes points out) that a single American institution, Indiana University, had 400 foreign citizens as members of its faculty for the year 1974–75, this is seen in proportion. As the International Research and Exchanges Board in its 1972–73 Report put it, 'Detente has not solved any fundamental problems of scholarly contact with the Soviet Union'.

Similarly, the immense number of man-hours devoted in Washington and Moscow to discussions on cultural and student exchanges has resulted in about twenty-five Soviet students working in the USA out of some 100,000 foreign students there. The number of students from Luxembourg is considerably greater, yet few meetings or conferences seem to have been held about Luxembourg-American cultural exchanges.

Many people believe that the importing of technology implies the importing of ideas. No doubt, a certain penumbra of unorthodox thought may penetrate with technological trading, but it seems unlikely that this peripheral seepage has a tangible effect on, or presents a noticeable threat to, the ruling *apparat*.

There is nothing new in this. Russia's rulers have always aimed to import Western technology for the purpose of strengthing the old system—especially in the military field. Such were the principles and practices of Peter the Great, Catherine the Great, and Stalin the (in his own way) equally Great. On each occasion the influx of Western techniques, though inseparable from a minor drift of ideas, was accompanied by an intensification of serfdom and a general tightening of despotism. Western technology was imported, while the Western political and civic principles which had made it possible were excluded. So Russia often had sophisticated armaments (as in the 1820s) but always fell behind later and needed yet more Western expertise.

Moreover, in trade and other non-military negotiations it is clear that the Soviets have virtually nothing we want. While the Kremlin is fully conscious of its need for Western computers and, on occasion, for Western wheat, it has very little, economically speaking, to give in exchange.

Genuine improvements in trade with the Soviet bloc are certainly desirable, though it is quite clear that they can never be more than marginal in the context of world trade, and vast inter-bloc trading booms are a vain hope. But if such trade serves merely to strengthen the Kremlin's ill-will towards the West, and to preserve the enormous armoury with which it is equipped, it is worse than useless. In any case the expansion of trade and political relaxation do not necessarily go together; for example Russo-German trade reached its peaks in 1913 and 1940 respectively, and when the USA recognised the USSR in1930, trade between the two countries declined throughout the following decade to a level of less than one sixth of what it had been before.

As Professor Walter Laqueur has noted, during World War II various economic experts in America predicted (in the words of Mr. Eric Johnston, then President of the Chamber of Commerce), that 'Russia will be, if not our biggest, at least our most eager customer when the war ends', (*Nation's Business*, October 1944). He was supported by a poll carried out by *Fortune* Magazine in 1945, which showed that business executives had more faith in Soviet post-war intentions than any other group in the American population. The same magazine (January 1945) estimated that US exports to the USSR would range between one and two billion dollars, while the US Bureau of Foreign and Domestic Commerce had suggested (in October 1943) that not less than a third of American exports would go to Russia after the war. In fact, US exports to Russia during the post-war period were much less than 1 per cent of the total.

It is odd to read continually about the importance of such trade relations with the West when, for example, German trade with the Benelux countries will (as Laqueur remarks) 'always be ten times bigger than trade with the Soviet Union'.

During a previous period of international 'thaw', Dr. Ronald Hingley noted that in his experience in Moscow, those most easily duped—even as to the evidence of their own eyes—were Western businessmen and scientists. We must hope that Western policy will not be influenced any longer by such people, or by the prospect of vast increases in trade; although some Western political leaders take a sadly short-sighted view of this matter. The West will always be at a disadvantage in trade with the USSR because we operate on a spontaneous, laissez-faire basis, as against the Soviet government monopoly of foreign trade and an effectively nonconvertible ruble. The establishment of a form of clearing house in the UK to help those who want to trade with the Soviet bloc would improve the situation.

Moreover trade with the USSR should not be aid. It is absurd to make arrangements by which Russia takes ten to twenty years to pay for Western products delivered now. The Russians could perfectly well pay, but for their own policies: if the Soviet Union reduced its defence budget to Western levels it could pay cash for the products it now buys on credit. It is the disproportionate effort that goes into armaments which distorts and even ruins the rest of the Soviet economy. While this is the case, Western aid amounts, in effect, to subsidising armaments designed to destroy the West. It would be short-sighted indeed to make trade 'the first priority' as some Western statesmen have urged, if the Soviet aim is simply the traditional one of seeking a breathing space of (as Peter the Great said in similar circumstances) going to the West for technical assistance only to turn Russia's backside on the West afterwards. The first priority must, on the contrary, be to ensure that trade—especially assistance in basic technical reconstruction—should move in step with the gaining of more fundamental advantages for the West and for world peace. If it seems that in five or ten years time, Russia will be revived and reinvigorated by Western aid, but still fully devoted in principle to the destruction of the West, an adult Western policy must strive to ensure the contrary—no reinvirgoration without relaxation.

Influential Westerners suggest that any attempt to sustain our own position, even verbally, will antagonise the Russians. This is based on a total misconception of Soviet motives. They have always wanted to have their cake and eat it, but they have never done anything they did not want to do because of Western politeness; and since they will continue to act solely in what they conceive to be their own interests, they will seek disarmament (for instance) only as far as they really want to disarm.

Naturally they are angry at no longer having everything their own way. The idea that the West has as much right to its ideals and interests as they have to theirs is quite contrary to their whole way of thinking. In other words they are irreconcilably opposed to us, and are not to be won over by psychological, economic, or other forms of appeasement. On the contrary, they will only act in ways we regard as desirable if we make it disadvantageous for them to do otherwise.

The concept of 'national interest' is alien to the mind of Russian despotism, and was so during the rule of the Tsars. Russian relations with foreigners were for centuries primarily a matter of conquering and absorbing bordering peoples, and there was no concept of a stable world order in which Russia would simply play its part. The post-revolutionary rulers, more than their predecessors, have a cultural background which gives them no reason to feel part of a broader international community. In fact, we may say that the Soviet Union does not in the ordinary sense conduct foreign policy—since, for the ruling group in Moscow, foreign countries are in principle either enemies or satellites. The idea of mutually respected common interests is absent.

In part, this is traditional or 'cultural'. But it has been taken to unprecedented extremes by the Leninist concept of politics—

that all other parties and movements are in principle to be regarded as hostile to Communism. Not only are Republicans and Conservatives, Democrats and Social-Democrats, Anarchists and Trotskyites, regarded as enemies to be out-manoeuvred and finally crushed, but also a number of Communist Parties have also shown themselves to be in a 'hostile camp'. The only part of the entire spectrum in world politics which is now regarded as reliable consists simply of the CPSU itself and those parties actually under its physical control. Just as under Lenin and Stalin, this principle of hostility and irreconcilability is still compatible with manoeuvres, truces, adjustments and temporary arrangements of every sort. Yet periods of negotiation with the Western 'capitalist' powers are seen as times to tighten up party discipline and ideological purity, rather than as reasons for relaxation.

It is difficult for the Western mind to understand this attitude. But there is also a tendency in the West to avoid facing the harsh realities at the centre of world problems. This may be natural enough. Years of crises and endless vigilance have taken their toll. There are many who wish to be deceived, who hope that the situation is not as difficult as it looks, 'for how unpleasant if it were'. Moreover, some feel that frank reporting and critical judgement of the USSR is harmful to international understanding.

Such people argue that by renouncing the voluntary expression of our own views and avoiding mention of Soviet blemishes, we may forward the cause of international understanding. Quite plainly the opposite is true. First, no lasting peace could be founded on the acceptance and propagation of a false view of one of the major powers on the international scene. But, secondly, the Communist powers will always pursue their own interest, regardless of whether they are criticised or exposed in the Western media. On the contrary, the more they can inculcate a favourable view of their intentions in the West, the more they feel able to press on regardless; in so far as Stalin's 'peace campaign' was effective, it increased his less peaceful tendencies, and strengthened his hand in the ensuing actions.

Is the Cold War over? We are given two different answers, often by the same prople. First, that it is over; second, that it is not but that it ought to be. Which shows that there is something peculiar about the whole idea. For what is (or alternatively, was) the Cold War? It is above all a metaphorical expression, one of the phrases which Orwell classed as simple, prefabricated parts for simple, prefabricated minds; and an assembly of them in varying shapes and proportions can give such a mind the idea that he is talking about, or even analysing, the realities of international politics.

Moreover, it is a prefabrication which can be used to mean two different things. First, a condition of international tension; and second, the expression of any opinion or fact unpalatable to the Soviet government. And since the same word is used for each these phenomena, it seems to imply to a vast section of the liberal audience that whoever offends under meaning (b) can automatically be charged under meaning (a).

Let us, then distinguish, and treat the two usages separately. 'Cold War', in the sense of extreme Soviet-Western tension, is usually applied to the period of Stalin's last years, the time of the Greek Civil War, the first Berlin blockade and the war in Korea. There is no quantitative measurement by which one can say that the Cold War is over. If any relaxation of its tensions is taken as ending it, then one might have said that the agreement ending the Berlin blockade in 1949 marked its close, at least temporarily. But if we take the view that in Stalin's time the Soviet Union was totally committed to a struggle with the West by all means short of major international war, and that this epoch has since expired, we must ask ourselves two questions. First, has the Soviet leadership really abandoned the principle of permanent conflict with the non-Communist powers? And second, if not, does it maintain the principle as a matter of doctrine, while in practice ceasing from activities likely to provoke trouble?

We should note that a period of decreased tension cannot in itself be taken to mean an essential, as against a tactical, change of policy. The non-expansion of the Soviet Union over the decade prior to 1939 was interpreted in this way; but it was due to weakness and lack of opportunity rather than to any change of principle.

After the Soviet invasion of Czechoslovakia in 1968, a number of commentators remarked that the Cold War had recommenced; they thought that the Soviet leaders had changed their policies for the worse. But the policies had not changed. The invasion only came as a surprise and shock to those who had let themselves be deluded about the whole question of Soviet motivations and policy. If reality is uncomfortable, it is nonetheless reality. And, plainly, any tendency in the West to see Russia in a deceptive light may be comforting for the moment but may also be lethal in the long run. Attempts at international harmony based on the repression or distortion of any information or opinion unwelcome to the ruling party in the USSR would be hollow, jerry-built and generally unreliable. The clearer the view we take about Russian affairs, the more firmly we express our own opinions, the better chance we have of attaining the greatest degree of international understanding possible today.

The Soviet press continues to run a constant propaganda campaign of the lowest sort against the Western countries. A series of untrue atrocity stories against the British Army in Northern Ireland continues unabated, together with highly detailed allegations about secret American cooperation in South African nuclear weapon development, about former Nazi experts helping the Israeli general staff, about large fees paid by British and American intelligence to Soviet democrats, and about West German (!) plots against Czechoslovak independence. It is important to remember that every word of this is written on behalf of the Communist Party of the Soviet Union and is checked and passed for publication by the highly rigorous state censorship organs. A single word from the Politburo would stop it. When Stalin arranged detente with Hitler in 1939–41, the Soviet press completely ceased to criticise Nazi Germany—even the word 'fascism' was banned. It operates today under precisely the same controls.

The link between international affairs and the published word is not that the Soviet leaders will be reasonable so long as nothing is said to their discredit; but that the test of genuine long-term relaxation, as against a truce based on considerations of power merely, is a lack of resentment at the publication of unpleasant truths. We in the West, do not suppress even the more unpleasant untruths and more hostile opinions put about by the Russians and their friends. So it is not even a question of truth or falsehood, but of the free movement of information and ideas.

Meanwhile, the term 'Cold War', applied to smear Western comment and research, should be banned from civilised discourse, or at least recognised as a despicable attempt to confuse important issues. Wherever this phrase is found, it may be taken as a touchstone of at best muddleheadedness, at worst active hostility to the principles of our culture.

If the Soviet rulers have really changed their attitudes and intentions, this is a very important development, and we should be provided with some evidence of the fact; those who claim that we should base our policy on this supposition should be required to prove it.

I would argue that they have not shown us such proofs and have rarely tried to do so. Their arguments are usually prefaced by such phrases as, 'we can assume . . .,' or 'in present world conditions it would be unreasonable of the Russians to . . .' And the evidence they produce is twofold. First, that 'things have changed' since Stalin. This is certainly true of some 'things', mainly internal. The regime now persecutes its critics rather than a random selection of the population, but the principles of rule have not changed. And with regard to foreign affairs it is difficult to think of an important fact which represents anything other than a tactical shift, for there is little significance in a few minor gestures, or occasional peaceable words.

Misapprehension about Soviet aims in certain Western circles has developed into a theoretical approach in the work of some academics. It has been said that you can find an academic to prove anything. Anyway a serious-sounding but essentially sophistical argument has been developed to support the view that the Russians mean no harm, or that if they do they cannot inflict it. The West is said to be so much more advanced technologically and in every other way that it cannot lose. As Professor Seton Watson has pointed out, man is a far more advanced species than the crocodile, but he would be ill-advised to rely on this while swimming in the Ganges. According to another argument, although the Kremlin once wished to extend its system over the world, it has now abandoned the project. Evidence is needed to support this proposition, and there is none. It is contrary to Soviet theory and it is contrary to Soviet practice. If they ever do change, we have quite clear criteria for testing the nature of the change.

A different form of intellectual confusion arises among those who admit that vigilance and firmness are needed, but who devise verbal formulae to misrepresent appeasement as its opposite. For example, we are told that the acceptance of Soviet nuclear superiority is a form of equality of deterrence, and, especially in American circles, a number of theories have been developed about Soviet overseas expansionism, which disguise appeasement and inaction as forms of sophisticated 'containment' in which Western liberty and world peace are preserved without taking much trouble.

As a result of such attitudes the situation has deteriorated dramatically over the past two or three years. First, and most basic, the American advantage in armaments has been largely lost. Second, a cycle of appeasement has set in, starting with the failure to give air support against the first probing attacks by the Vietnamese Communists early in 1975, the failure to act in Angola, and the lack of serious opposition to the establishment of a Soviet puppet state in Ethiopia. This can only encourage the Kremlin to further adventures.

The most disturbing point is not merely the absence of appropriate or adequate action in these fields, but the West's continued practice of its conception of detente in fields advantageous to the Soviet Union while permitting hostile Soviet action where that happens to suit the Kremlin. Even if Western intervention in Angola or Ethiopia were not plausible, at least these ostentatious adventures could be countered by the suspension of technological cooperation with the USSR.

And so we are entering a decade of great international danger. If the Soviet leaders were ever to find themselves in a position where they thought they could destroy the American nuclear strike capability, there could be no question of trusting them not to take us at least to the edge of the nuclear holocaust.

4

Arms

In the present situation the subject of armaments, and the appropriate level of Western arms, has become a central issue of foreign policy.

I have argued that the most serious task facing us must be the avoidance on the one hand of nuclear war, and on the other of the overthrow of the Western democratic culture by its regressive despotic opponents. Each implies that the disincentives to aggression must be so clear that no misunderstanding is possible. This in turn means an armaments policy which leaves the USSR in no doubt whatever of their inability to win a nuclear war. The industrial power of the West is so much greater than that of the Soviet bloc, and its technological superiority equally evident, that there is no material reason why this aim should not be achieved.

The economic potential of the West in gross national product is also far greater than that of the Soviet Union. The GNP of the NATO countries (and France) in 1977 was 3,367 billion dollars against the Warsaw Pact's 1,240 billion dollars. And that is to say nothing of the other allies and friends of the West: Australia, New Zealand, Japan, Spain, and Brazil add another 864 billion. The contribution of Russia's allies outside the Warsaw Pact is negligible. Even the population of the NATO countries is greater, with 554.8 million against the Warsaw Pact's 365.7 million. And, with all the deficiencies of the Western effort, military manpower is not much less than that of the Pact; 4.8 million as against 5.2 million.

In a direct comparison between the US and the USSR, the Soviet GNP in 1978 was about 1,200 billion as against the American 2,000 billion (and for a larger population). Nevertheless, the USSR finds it necessary to match the United States in armaments, with something like 13 per cent of its GNP devoted to military expenditure against 5.1 per cent of the American GNP. Soviet military expenditure is, moreover, continually increasing by about 4 per cent per annum. For the last ten or fifteen years the USSR has devoted the highest possible proportion of its energy and resources to a single-minded programme of increasing its armament, and making it ever more effective. This effort has not been matched by the West, with the result that the balance has shifted in favour of our opponents.

Those who warn of Soviet advances towards and beyond parity with the United States are said to be in error because America has 'a substantial technological lead', but that is not much use unless it is actually translated into weapons.

Recent years have seen a gradual but unceasing retreat; at first US superiority was necessary, then parity was sufficient and finally inferiority was acceptable so long as the criteria of mutual force destruction were met. Each shift left the situation more precarious, and the safety margin smaller, till now, in the judgement of many, that margin is dangerously thin. None of this has been inevitable. It has been the result of policy decisions based on argument, and the desire to satisfy sentiment among an influential minority who are opposed to armaments and reluctant to face unpleasant facts.

A recent report by an American study group suggests that neither side could in any 'real sense' win a nuclear war, because of the enormous physical and human losses involved. But that is to evade the point! Although it wishes to avoid a nuclear war the Soviet Union may well calculate that in the event it might be able to inflict more damage than it suffered, and still dispose of sufficient organization and force to occupy its opponents' territory. Examination of all recent Soviet writings on military doctrine indicate that the pervading idea is that they might indeed 'win' such a war. These Soviet studies are dismissed by appeasers in the West as 'merely' reflecting what the military think: but accepted military opinion is bound to influence political attitudes. As Edward N. Luttwak notes (*Commentary*, January 1978),

'Above all, the United States has misused arms control in the attempt to dampen the strategic competition in itself, as if the growth of strategic arsenals were the cause of Soviet-American rivalry rather than merely one of its symptoms . . . .

On the SALT negotiations some prominent American Senators feel that it is essential to avert the danger of war by securing an agreement between the great nuclear powers. Otherwise (they argue) there would be an extremely expensive arms race. Unfortunately, this implies acceptance of the principle that an agreement is so valuable that its content is secondary. For example, the original SALT proposals made early in 1977 represented a reasonably sound American minimum position. When they were rejected by the USSR, evidently on the calculation that political pressures in the West would be exerted to weaken them, retreat did indeed take place. It seems now that the Soviet Union and agreement-fetishists in the West mean to settle for the worst bargain that the US Senate can be persuaded to accept by every combination of baseless assurance and verbal confusion.

There has been considerable unease in Europe also, about the recent state of the SALT negotiations. The USA, which builds, pays for and, to a large extent, mans the weaponry involved might regard it as peculiarly its own concern. But the defence of the West is a complex and interlocking business, in which a failure to match Soviet arms in the ICBM field, for example, has instant repercussions on the necessity for weapons capable of stopping Soviet tanks on the Elbe. Of course, we ourselves could do more, and such an effort is in a sense a condition of our influence in the alliance. All the same, when there is any doubt about American willpower, the desire for national deterrents is bound to arise as it has in France. Nor is this either illogical or unreasonable.

The former American negotiator no SALT, Mr. Paul Warnke, was regarded by most of the Senate as insufficiently hard-headed about the Russians and was only confirmed by an admittedly reluctant majority after the hope was expressed that he would take a firmer line. A member of his team is quoted (*US News and World Report*, 23 January 1978) as saying, 'He is supremely confident he can talk the Russians into making sharp cuts later on in their missile strength simply to contribute to

stability—but the Kremlin doesn't believe in unilateral disarmament'.

The problems in American foreign policy over the past year
seem to be due to conceptual errors by some of that interesting
and comparatively small community of academics and others,
who make up what is sometimes known as 'the foreign policy
establishment'. Mr. Warnke himself has now been transferred,
but he is wholly typical of this element, a number of whom now
hold posts among the top appointments in the State Department . . .

It is true to say that the Soviet leaders want peace, but only
to the extent compatible with the eventual destruction of our
political system, and insofar as it preserves their own. It is also
important to note that the possession of a great nuclear arsenal
enables the USSR to 'lean' politically on states in its vicinity.
The increase in Soviet arms has not been confined to nuclear
weapons, but also includes increases in tanks, naval forces,
and troop transport planes able to deploy its ground troops far
afield. The 'external function' of the Soviet armed forces has
been well defined by the head of their main political administration, General A. A. Yepishev (a former Deputy Minister of
Stalin's Secret Police): 'Socialism's military might objectively
assists the successful development of the revolutionary, liberation movements'. Or, to put it in Western terms, we cannot
implement sound and firm international policies with any
assurance, unless our military power is adequate to outface the
Kremlin. Strong political leadership and will-power are vital in
this situation. In a democratic electorate there is supposed
reluctance to spend large sums on 'useless' things like arms,
though we are willing to pay for equally 'unproductive' expenses
like insurance for the home, or lifeboats on ocean liners. But
it is a reluctance which responds to proofs of necessity. Those
who oppose armaments for a variety of reasons, from sympathy
with the Communist states to comfortable delusions about their
aims, may have some influence on the public, but the latter has
a welcome capacity to face facts and ask for right decisions—
more so, indeed, than many of its alleged mentors.

Political leaders in the United Kingdom and the United
States no longer have the excuse that their electorate would
not support a higher level of armament. Polls in Britain have

shown that the majority understand the danger and accept the need for an increase in armaments. Such is also the case in America, where even high school students have polled favourably on this issue. A recent poll showed that 48 per cent of the US public believe that the United States should be superior in military strength to the Soviet Union, and 42 per cent that it should be about equal (3 per cent wanted the US to be inferior). 63 per cent of that public are willing to spend an additional 10 billion dollars a year—even if it means a tax increase—in order to assure equality with or superiority to the Soviet Union. (64 per cent think that the Russians would not keep any agreement they signed on limiting strategic weapons, while 18 per cent think they would).

From Britain's point of view, it is worth emphasizing that the GNP of the Western European members of the North Atlantic Alliance, without the USA and Canada, greatly exceeds that of the whole Warsaw Pact *including* the USSR. The theory that it would be *impossible* for Europe to defend itself against the USSR and its allies, if America for any reason became unable to help, is invalid.

The United States has high technology plus brute economic power. The USSR has, by the totalitarian channelling of every possible source into the military field, matched and outmatched that power. While the potential economic strength of Western Europe greatly exceeds that of the USSR, it is not similarly deployable. On the other hand, Western Europe uses high technology to almost the same extent as America. The advent of cheaper but more sophisticated weapons like the cruise missile thus gives a great advantage, in principle at least, to the European arms programme. As long as we have any doubt about the American position, we should develop our own advanced weapons.

In general, we should press ahead with technological development in which the West is well in advance of the USSR, but which the United States is not pursuing for one reason or another. That is, of course, when it is within our capacity and resources to do so. We still have very fine research and development capabilities which are not always adequately employed. Some years ago the Americans abandoned the NERVA project for developing a nuclear rocket engine, though this had reached a fairly advanced stage. I was assured at the time by British rocket engineers that our own underemployed resources would have been ideally suited to developing this project, which concerned a new generation of engines, two or three times as powerful as present ones, and would have enabled us to leapfrog to the front in aerospace development. This may still be the case.

If American armaments appear barely adequate it becomes all the more necessary for the United Kingdom (and the other NATO allies) to increase our own strength. At the same time we should use our influence with the Americans to get them to step up their programme, and if we ourselves were doing so, this would add weight to our argument. For the best solution for the alliance must be a far more strongly coordinated strategic and tactical arms policy.

We must realise that there is a certain danger of the Russians seizing the opportunities presented them by a period in which they have effective superiority, and there is no doubt that they will use every diplomatic and propaganda weapon to prevent a build-up of Western strength to adequate levels. It will require a strong political nerve to handle this situation but the alternative is to acquiesce in the increasing debilitation of our defences, and this carries far greater dangers with it.

Meanwhile, we must remember that our security is and has been preserved by the policy of deterrence. It would be admirable to have international agreements limiting but not compromising the deterrent. But we can have the deterrent without the agreement; and we can have the agreement without the deterrent. Given the choice, weapons are a sounder defence than paper.

5

Human Rights

Our first duty to freedom is (as Mrs. Thatcher has well said) to keep our own. To do this we must see that freedom's greatest enemies do not increase their sway. Just as in the last war, we must find our allies where we may, while encouraging them to be more democratic. At one time our only effective ally was the Greek military dictatorship, and later we relied on Stalin himself. In that way, while almost the whole of Europe was under totalitarian rule in 1941 and 1942, now at least half is free.

If the progress of liberty in the world is complex, the same may be said of the evolution of particular countries; the transition to freedom is not an easy one. The experience of Portugal, so long on the verge of a takeover by new, Communist dictators, should remind us of that.

We know, too, that the existence of complete freedom in itself may sometimes lead to fearful tyrannies, if freedom's enemies are strong. The Nazi and Communist despots both came to power in conditions of almost total liberty. (As Alexander Solzhenitsyn has reminded us, the liberties Russia enjoyed for a few months in 1917 had to be paid for by sixty years of totalitarian dictatorship.) Liberty can only flourish under the protection of law, guaranteed by a state which is strong because it preserves rights rather than intruding on them, strong in its reliance on the community as a whole. To demand liberty without this safeguard is to demand an anarchy which must lead to despotism. Those of the extreme Left make such excessive demands for 'rights' that the state would be left with little authority, and yet are friendly towards some very rigid dictatorships. This is natural, for anarchy is but the obverse of tyranny. Each tends to produce the other, and each

55

is equally far removed from the real complexities of a society which is based on consensus.

There are many countries where the immediate choice is not between political liberty and dictatorship, but between total, fanatical dictatorship and a more temporary, emergency regime, from which political liberty might later emerge. We ourselves recognise that there are occasions when rights have to be suspended: the Riot Act is one such example, and there are occasions in all Western countries when martial law or a state of emergency is accepted as necessary to preserve the democratic state as a last resort in maintaining the order without which liberty must perish.

M. Pierre Trudeau, a man with a reputation for liberalism, was faced in 1970 by a wave of terrorism (although it was less severe than recent examples elsewhere.) A British diplomat was kidnapped and a Canadian Minister kidnapped and shot by the French Canadian separatist group F.L.Q. He immediately took firm action and condemned critics as people who believed in

> a veto by a few guys who want to throw bombs. If that is allowed to happen, it's the end of freedom in this country.

Large numbers of troops were sent in to guard buildings and public figures, and emergency laws were invoked. Trudeau said to reporters,

> Society must defend itself. There are a lot of bleeding hearts around who don't like to see people with helmets and guns. All I can say is—go on and bleed.

If a country is totally disrupted by so-called 'urban guerillas', are we really to condemn out of hand a reversion to military rule, when that may be the only alternative? It is a matter of judgement. We cannot say that such action is justified in every case, but at least the context must be taken into account. I do not think we could have objected if the German Army had intervened to prevent Hitler's quite constitutional access to power, as some of its leaders wished. We may feel that a state like South Korea is a similar case—facing a ruthless enemy across a precarious border. It is easy to condemn from a safe distance. We ourselves suspended our usual civil rights to imprison Fascists without trial in 1940, and suppressed publications giving comfort to the enemy—and who shall blame us?

Here I must counter the old argument that partial and temporary restrictions on liberty occur even in the Western democracies and that therefore it is wrong to talk of 'the free world', or to censure Soviet oppressions. The answer of course is that nothing in real life comes in a pure state: but there is a basic difference between drinking a glass of brine and a glass of fresh water, even though the latter, far from being a pure distillation, contains a sensible proportion of salts. Some liberty is better than none: people do not normally thank society for allowing them to breathe, but in the gas ovens of Auschwitz, or even the black hole of the Lubyanka, it was different.

We might make other distinctions. A new regime which represses active and dangerous enemies may relax when the immediate crisis is over, and is less reprehensible than a regime which continues the same oppression after decades. A regime which massacres whole social or racial groups, as in Uganda and Cambodia today, and in Hitlerite Germany and Stalinist Russia yesterday, is worse than one which destroys specified political opponents. A regime which represses armed terrorists is not in the same category as one which represses unarmed writers. Public attention is not necessarily drawn to the worst atrocities. This is partly because a really closed totalitarian regime can prevent its crimes becoming known—as in North Korea and Communist Vietnam. Mrs. Nadezhda Mandelstam, widow of the great Russian poet murdered by Stalin, tells us that things got worse in the USSR when the terror disappeared from the streets.

Meanwhile there is only one enemy of liberty which has built up the power to threaten the very existence of political civilization on this planet. It is not Chile or China which has a vast and increasing armament, and is behind anti-Western moves everywhere; it is Russia. We live in a world where only a couple of dozen countries enjoy a broad measure of human rights. Does this mean that we should abandon the other half of the world to freedom's major foes? Of course not.

Two principles emerge by which we may judge a repressive regime: first, is it an ally and accomplice of the main threat to world liberty? second, is its repression due to local and temporary causes, or does it justify itself as a permanent part of the state? Until a few decades ago, it was generally assumed in the more backward parts of the world that political democracy was the most advanced type of state. Countries which remained wholly or partly dictatorial nevertheless accepted that this was due to the temporary circumstance of backwardness, and aspired in principle to a more democratic condition. Forms of parliamentary democracy were initiated and when the armed forces intervened (as in Turkey), they usually restored a degree of democracy after a short period. More recent dictators, however, no longer apologise and urge their temporary nature. On the contrary, inspired by the justificatory jargon of Leninism, they represent permanent dictatorship as in itself desirable, and superior to 'bourgeois democracy'.

We may distinguish between regimes which have come to power by an act of violence, and those which make violence a permanent principle of rule. Despotism is a primitive phase, however modern the words used to disguise it. It represents the childish notion that all problems can be solved by willpower, by orders from above. As Edmund Burke pointed out in a famous passage, and as we can see throughout the Communist world, despotic rulers fail to get results by the endless application of force. They do not solve the problems, they merely suppress them. And the problems return to haunt them, ever more insoluble.

There are cases where we must make allowances. But this should never leave our central position unclear: we must stand for liberty. The United Kingdom is going through a relatively bad period at present: but that is no reason for not to insisting that our system is incomparably superior, by every test, to the ideological tyranny and political primitivism of the one-party state. Even our present comparative poverty represents inconceivable prosperity by the standards of the socialist dictatorships of the Soviet bloc.

Whatever allowances we may make for the difficulties of a country in a state of emergency, whatever our need to establish alliance against the principal threat, we must always hold to our basic principles. In some cases we may accept dictatorship as a temporary expedient; it is not for the West to decree the speed and method of movement towards democracy. But we must never countenance the idea that the absence of liberty can be justified for its own sake.

When considering the human rights issue we must remember that no other political culture really cares about it, but that under the rules of 'doublethink', they have to pretend that they do, and devise a special vocabulary for this purpose. Hypocrisy has often been used in defence of vice throughout human history but has never been entirely successful. And so, in this field, we have a great advantage: all we need to do is tell the truth and cut through obfuscation.

The human rights issue is crucial to the relationship between ourselves and the Soviet Union. In that country undesirable political, economic, or religious ideas are suppressed; those who express them are persecuted by imprisonment, pseudo-psychiatric treatment and expulsion from the country; foreign books and periodicals are banned; the million Crimean Tatars, Meskhetians, and Volga Germans are exiled from their homelands; and the Jews are harassed. All this is profoundly distasteful to those who cherish the principles of Western culture. But there is more to it than that. President Kennedy was perceptive when he said: 'peace, in the last analysis, is a matter of human rights'.

There are areas of the world in which tyranny, however distasteful, is not a direct threat to the West; others where a despotic regime lacks the power to harm us, or—itself under threat—might arguably help us. In these areas the question is purely a moral one. However, in the USSR human rights do not concern us simply as a matter of principle, but also directly affect our own interests. In this context I shall concern myself less with the humanitarian aspect of the problem than with its profound significance for Western foreign policy.

For here we have a simple test of the way in which the Soviet leaders regard democratic and other ideas which we hold to be central to the Western culture. When those who hold these ideas and wish to express them are inside the USSR, they are bullied, arrested, sent to forced labour camps, or subjected to 'psychiatric' torture. If this is what they do to democrats who are helpless before the power of the KGB, this must be the treatment they regard as appropriate for democrats everywhere,

whenever possible. The profound Soviet hostility to reconciliation and peace with the West is shown above all by the
suppression of Western-style thought in the USSR, and the
imposition there of the thesis that it must also be fought
elsewhere in the world. Their basic motive remains the destruction of all other political life-forms. In the meanwhile, they will
use whatever manoeuvres in diplomatic and other relationships
are expedient.

It is in this context that we should consider the question of
human rights in the USSR. Above all, it constitutes the great
test of their true attitudes. This understanding, particularly on
the part of certain Northern European leaders, led to the in-
clusion in the 1975 Helsinki Agreement of 'Basket Three',
which was concerned with the free movement of people and
ideas, and emphasised the liberty of the subject and freedom of
thought.

Of the two, the first, though of vital importance, does not
have the scope of the second. Unfortunately the principle of
free movement has become reduced in many Western minds to
free emigration of Jews (who are of course not specified in
either the Helsinki Agreement or the Jackson Amendment);
nevertheless that principle is an indispensable last sanction by
any of the oppressed against the claims of the state, and once
secured would be enormous first step towards civilizing Russia.
But the free movement of ideas is more fundamental. When
Milton wrote 'Give me the liberty to know, to utter, and to
argue freely according to conscience, above all liberties', he
implied that while freedom of thought does not contain all the
other things we would list as human rights, it contains their
potential, and they cannot be realized or sustained without it.
The free movement of ideas is not some parochial fad of
Western culture. It distinguishes a society with the possibility of
peaceful change and progress from one without it. It distinguishes an articulated social order, with its compromise and
consensus, from a barracks or a prison. It distinguishes a
country able to tolerate different ideas and forms of state in
others, from one based on the principle of the imposition everywhere of received truth. It constitutes, in fact, all that is meant
by political civilization; and it sets the standard for an essentially peaceable state.

The Final Act at Helsinki asserted flatly that

> The participating States recognize the universal significance of human rights and fundamental freedoms, respect for which is an essential factor for the peace, justice and well-being necessary to ensure the development of friendly relations and co-operation among themselves as among all States.

'Basket Three' of the agreement was an attempt to get from the Russians, in exchange for other concessions, an implementation of these general points and the beginning of a free movement of people and ideas; the West had no other political demands. It will be noted that we asked no more than we already grant: Communist ideas circulate freely in the West and Western citizens can move freely about Europe. Nor did our negotiators make any unreal demands for immediate and total fulfilment of these points: the terms of the agreement were 'gradually to simplify and to administer flexibly the procedure for exit and entry', 'to ease regulations', 'gradually to lower', 'gradually to increase' (just as the Jackson Amendment asked for a relaxation of the restrictions on emigration, not instant freedom). Indeed, Helsinki was a most modest start, just seeking a sign of the beginnings of Soviet tolerance towards their own citizens, even those who may not share the ideas of their government or accept its claim to control their every move.

Helsinki was intended to inaugurate a new epoch of good will. In Russia itself we would be seeing, had its provisions been carried out,

> the effective exercise of civil, political, economic, social, cultural and other rights and freedoms all of which derive from the inherent dignity of the human person and are essential for his free and full development.

The representatives of the USSR 'solemnly' bound their government to these propositions. No attempt has been made to fulfil these obligations. In the West few lessons have been drawn, during a period in which our own political sense and political will have deteriorated. It seems to be assumed that reasonable people could hardly expect the Russians to carry out their duties, however solemnly undertaken.

In the USSR itself more than one imprisoned Soviet dissident has pleaded that the Soviet acceptance of the Helsinki Agreement and the UN Declaration of Human Rights should mean their immediate release, only to have the interrogator say 'That is not for us. That is for Blacks'—in other words, for Blacks as long as they remain beyond Soviet influence. We are told by the unanimous voice of the Soviet dissenters that things would be even worse if it were not for the vigilant eyes with which Soviet excesses are watched in the West. Ironically, because the Russians do not wish to destroy entirely their reputation among the most stubborn dupes in the West, and want to use certain elements in the West for their own political purposes, they are showing what is for them comparative restraint. They have not shot dissenters, using instead starvation rations and psychiatric torture. But they have failed to grant any of the public freedoms they solemnly promised.

The best that can be said is that Soviet 'double talk' has been forced into the open, and the true position made quite clear. Moscow must either take the first steps towards real accomodation and reconciliation, or—if not—they will be unable any longer to deceive and entrap the world public by false pretences of peace and friendship. When the Soviet leaders persecute and silence a democrat who is in their power, they are declaring that democracy is unfit to live. They are branding as illegitimate non-Communist ideas and institutions everywhere. And they are establishing their right, when and if they have the power, to destroy the Western political culture, as they do its adherents on the spot.

Until this intolerance, this hatred of all other forms of political life is eroded, the danger to the world remains. When we consider that these are the motives behind the accumulation of the largest armament ever seen in Europe, the problem becomes urgent and vital. We must seek disarmament. But above all we must seek psychological disarmament. A siege mentality has prevailed too long in the Soviet block: and, it has been well said, a siege mentality is but the obverse of a sortie mentality. This is the unpleasant conclusion we must draw.

On the other hand, implementation of the Helsinki Agreement can be used to test of any evolution on the Russian part towards the toleration of other political forms in the world. As soon as they cease to persecute the Human Rights Movement in the USSR, we can regard it as a signal that they are prepared for the principle of toleration in the world as a whole. If and when ideas and people begin to move freely over the Soviet and Eastern European frontiers we will have a genuine sign that peaceful intentions are prevailing.

Until they do, we will know that the Soviet leaders remain in a state of irreconcilable hostility, with all the dangers that entails. With such a regime we can only seek as stable a truce as possible, based on mutual mistrust, and guaranteed on our side by eternal vigilance and a strong defence effort. Even that is better than delusions of friendship based on no more than a few fine words. But we must hope for better still. We must make the Kremlin understand that ingrained hatreds will lead nowhere, and that peace can only be served by some abatement, however, motivated, of active hostility. This will be no easy task, but if we set our minds to it, we may create the beginnings of a truly stable peace.

We must ask for internal tolerance because we see it as an essential part of the larger tolerance which is necessary if peace is to have a firm foundation. We ask only for some sign that their enmity to our world has become less absolute, less intransigent. We are not asking the Soviet leaders to give up their power. We are not even asking them to give up one-party rule. We ask for no more than the free movement of people and ideas. We ask for that liberty to emigrate which the Tsars granted without affecting their own power. And we ask, above all, for the free movement of ideas. If indeed the Communist idea is superior, as they claim, it should be able to prevail in free argument, especially after two generations of the population have been indoctrinated. We must ask for this freedom in the name of peace. To secure it should be the central aim of our whole policy towards the Soviet Union. They should gain no benefits, economic, technical or political from us except to the extent that they are willing to pay for them in the intangible coin of liberty and tolerance, the true dowry of peace.

Although the differences between political cultures are as persistent as they are profound, and they have an enormous intrinsic momentum, eventually they can be turned. Despotism has evolved in a more civic direction as in pre-revolutionary

Russia. Apart from a catastrophic breakdown, which is by no means impossible, slow and firm pressures and inducements from our side might eventually lead first to the abandonment in practice of the Soviet struggle to the knife with the West, and later to its abandonment even in principle. But our immediate situation is dangerous, and a policy of slow erosion through trade and cultural contacts, rather than serious attempts at political leverage, will be ineffective.

Ideologies do evolve—under pressure. When the disadvantages of pursuing aggressive policies are made clear, and the advantages to be gained by concession are continually present as a bait, only then is there a reasonable prospect of substantial change. Lack of firmness is a certain guarantee that the Kremlin, having no inducement to change, will continue its present policy of hostility in both principle and practice. So-called 'realists' argue that we cannot expect the Soviet rulers to make concessions and so should not press them to do so; this is to surrender in advance, encourage aggressiveness, and failing to prevent its continuation in the foreseeable future. One is tempted to say of them, as in another context, Orwell said of intellectuals who favoured appeasement, one doesn't know which to despise more, their cynicism or their short-sightedness. Any Western statesman who puts human rights clauses into a treaty and then makes no attempt to see that they are fulfilled seems to be collaborating with the Soviet Union in deceiving his own constituents. This is particularly the case if he cites Soviet willingness to accept such clauses as an authentic sign of change in the Kremlin. Indeed, the inculcation of such deluded ideas can only confuse and weaken the Western will to resist.

Our foreign policy should have the short term aim of preserving world peace between antagonistic cultures, and the long term hope of securing not just a truce, but a truly peaceful world. The way to achieve this is not through agressive crusading, but by example on the one hand and, on the other, by encouraging the evolution of despotic cultures from the economic, intellectual and civic stagnation which is the result of their present policies. Meanwhile we should try not to blur our basic intentions; for example, we should not encourage the more aggressive or expansionist Soviet tendencies by surrendering on small matters in which we have a genuine grievance, or issue of principle. Harsh public words are not required; firmness is. Theodore Roosevelt's much maligned advice is apposite: 'Speak softly but carry a big stick'.

The element of genuine detente in present international relations is not based on any Soviet acceptance of peace or permanent cooperation. It is ill-defined, variable and unstable. To exaggerate it is to do a disservice to peace.

More than thirty years ago Arthur Koestler wrote a remarkable article, which appeared in the *New York Times* (10 March 1946) and at the same time in the London weekly *Tribune*. In it he goes to the heart of the problem presented by the Soviet Union in world affairs. He says, in part,

> The first necessity is that our own statesmen should realise that no political treaties and trade agreements can guarantee peace as long as this world remains psychologically divided into two worlds, with persecution-mania on one side, growing alarm on the other. The conclusion and aim of this article is a plea to politicians for the inclusion of the psychological factor in their power-calculations, as a factor equal in importance to Air Forces and Navies ... Psychological armaments should be made an object of international negotiations and of political bargaining just as armaments in the air and on the sea; and made subject to as clearly defined clauses as, for instance, naval armaments are ... By 'psychological armaments' I do not mean criticism directed by one country against another. This democratic right is as vital on the international as on the national scale, and such criticism cannot do much harm if the country criticized has full facilities of stating its case before the public of the country from which the criticism comes. But it becomes poisonous if the country attacked is deprived of this right of defence—as the Western contries are at present in the Soviet Press ...
>
> The measure of 'psychological armament' is the extent to which a government obstructs the free exchange of information and ideas with the outside world. A country which builds a Maginot line of censorship from behind which it fires its propaganda salvoes is committing psychological aggression ...
>
> The Western Powers ... should ... demand ...
>
> > (a) free access of foreign newspapers, periodicals, books and films to the USSR;
> >
> > (b) such modifications of the Russian censorship (if censor-

ship there must be) as to permit the free circulation of
information about the outside world throughout Soviet
territory;

(c) free access for accredited journalists, parliamentary
committees, etc., to Russian-occupied territory;

(d) the abolishing of restriction on travel for foreigners in
Soviet territory, and for Soviet citizens abroad;

(e) active co-operation with the Western Powers in the
organization of 'vacations abroad' schemes, on a
mutual exchange basis, for students, teachers, writers,
workers, and professional men . . .

Nobody in his senses will expect the Soviet leaders to agree
to this easily. Hence the suggestion that psychological disarmament should be made a bargaining object in all future negotiations, and given high priority on the political agenda. The
demand for the free circulation of ideas across frontiers, for
restoring the arrested bloodstream of the world, should be
rasied at every meeting of the Big Three, the Security Council,
the Committees and Assembly of the United Nations; it should
be made the pre-condition of concessions in the geographical,
economical and scientific field. To get it accepted, the use of all
levers of pressure, political and economical, would for once be
morally justified.

What Koestler could see clearly nearly a third of a century
ago is still not plain to some Western statesmen. The central
idea comes up again—as in the Helsinki negotiations—and is
again left as a peripheral hope. It is time to recognize its
importance.

In conclusion, we would perhaps be best advised, while
watching for any favourable signs, to be under no illusions
about the present political culture of the USSR, the present
motivations of its leadership. The worst way to try to induce
even gradual change is to grant approval to the status quo.
Only when the Kremlin sees that its present attitudes are profit-
less might any inducement to change arise (if not among them
at least perhaps somewhere in the power-apparatus). Incentives
to change, disincentives to their present attitude—at any rate
that is the best we can do. Meanwhile a wary truce based on a
true and sober appreciation of their real feelings and aims may
not be very attractive; but it is better than euphoria based on
delusion.

6

Negotiation; Treaties; The United Nations

Foreign affairs are often represented by professionals as too subtle and intricate for the layman. In fact, there is nothing very difficult about the main principles of a foreign policy. The complications arise in the handling of comparatively minor details—though even these are simpler to manage if there is a clear general policy behind them.

On 1 August 1975, after two years of negotiation, the United Kingdom, the United States, European friends and allies, and the Soviet Union and its allies, together with the neutral European states, signed the Final Act of the Helsinki Conference. These countries declared themselves, in the words of the Act,

> Motivated by the political will, in the interest of peoples, to improve and intensify their relations and to contribute in Europe to peace, security, justice and co-operation as well as to rapprochement among themselves and with other States of the world, determined, in consequence, to give full effect to the results of the Conference and to assure, among their States and throughout Europe, the benefits deriving from those results and thus to broaden, deepen and make continuing and lasting the process of detente . . .

The Soviet Union has defaulted on that part of the Helsinki accord—the issue of human rights—from which the West and the world really stood to gain. As we noted, no serious attempt was made to secure Soviet compliance. The few token gestures they made on the issue, concerning individuals only, have been tacitly accepted by the Western advocates of detente who have effectively also defaulted on the Helsinki accord.

In obtaining Soviet signatures to international documents the West obtained nothing. The problem remains that of enforcement. Indeed, a signed guarantee which only applies when the USSR finds it convenient may prove the total unreliability of the Soviet signature to any document. (It is certainly true that Soviet-signed treaties guaranteeing the independence of the Baltic States and the toleration of all anti-fascist parties in the Balkan countries and East Germany, meant and mean nothing). Yet our negotiators probably did not insist on the provisos of 'Basket Three' being made watertight because they thought the USSR would not then sign; and they had some slight hope that vague phraseology might nevertheless produce some small result in exchange for substantial Western concessions on other issues. Now that we know this sort of bargain to be worthless, perhaps future negotiators will insist on terms of substance—or alternatively not sign meaningless documents whose only effect is to mislead Western opinion into thinking that genuine agreement has been reached.

The main Soviet defence of the indefensible is that to request that they observe their solemn undertaking is 'intervention' in their internal affairs. These liberties are indeed partly internal matters. But why, then, did the USSR enter freely into such guarantees if they did not mean to observe them? In the Western view, these matters had a major foreign policy significance, and the free movement of ideas is very much an international issue. For example, what of the undertaking

> To facilitate the improvement of the dissemination, on their territory, of newspapers and printed publications, periodical and nonperiodical, *from the other participating states* (my italics).

Needless to say, there has been no sign of this at all. The Soviet excuses are contemptible and reach new depths when they use the 'internal affairs' argument, for they themselves constantly intervene overtly in the internal affairs of other countries, such as South Africa, which they regard as legitimate subjects for their concern and action.

The fact remains, then, that the USSR has given solemn

undertakings, and made no effort at all to fulfil them. What can we conclude from this? That their signatures to an agreement are not worth the paper they are written on. If that is a fact of international life, then it is something we should recognize. It also follows that the Soviet leaders will do nothing they do not wish to do, however solemn their guarantees, unless we are in a position to make it disadvantageous for them to default.

As long as the Russians can get the trade they want, recognition of their conquests, and no interference with their expansionism, without having to make any concessions in exchange, they will continue as before. They will make no improvements on the vital issue of human rights unless we insist on it in return for any concession we make in other fields.

The Helsinki undertakings are absolutely clear, as are Soviet undertakings under the UN Declaration on Human Rights, and they have taken no steps whatsoever to fulfil them. Once again we gave them something they wanted—a legitimisation of their conquests in Eastern Europe—in exchange for an assorted batch of smiles and promises. Those who were sceptical of Soviet good will were once again proved right, and those sanguine people who believed that the Russian signature on these high-minded documents inaugurated a new age of peace, were proved to be simpletons. It is surprising that this lesson still needed to be learnt after decades of similar experiences.

For example, after the signature of an arms agreement, the rulers of the USSR will at once begin minor violations which may be regarded as probing moves. If they are not brought up sharply each time, they gradually increase the pressure to get more than they are allowed. These small violations are sometimes treated in the West as too unimportant to warrant any breach of the atmosphere of detente. They are themselves, of course, just such breaches: and, as soon as there is reliable evidence of such actions, we should suspend negotiations on every other issue.

Failure to offer such resistance led to the visits by Soviet ballistic missile submarines to Cuba, in violation of agreements to the contrary. These visits were gradually lengthened when there was no noticeable Western reaction. Supporting facilities were then built and these were only partly removed after American protests.

Similarly the 1972 interim agreement in connection with SALT-1 required the Russians to scrap equal numbers of older land-based missiles before taking new missile submarines to sea. They disregarded their promise: there were American complaints, but the Russians made a feeble excuse about the weather, and no more was said.

Much has been written on the special problems of negotiation with the USSR by many Westerners who have learned by bitter experience in this field. It is well-known that a Western concession on one issue will not buy a Soviet concession on the next issue and that if the Soviet negotiators believe that we want an agreement for its own sake, they will harden their demands to the maximum. It is always preferable to break off negotiations in these circumstances, and to let the Soviet Union know that this will be done, even if it means that no agreement will be concluded.

There is clearly a great advantage in diplomatic positions which are, as it were, self-enforcing. The advantage of the Jackson amendment is that it insisted on a human right with safeguards against non-fulfilment. It did not grant benefits without a mechanism for checking on Soviet performance of their side of the bargain. In these cases, if the Russians comply, well and good. If not, we have avoided giving something for nothing, and the inducement to more civilized and peaceable conduct remains. Russia has never had a tradition that trade or negotiation can lead to mutual benefit: the first true merchant bank in the country was only founded in the 1860s and the Communist contribution to this outlook was the usual principle 'Who-Whom'?: the idea that every act is part of a struggle in which one side loses and the other wins.

No unified theory of foreign policy tactics is possible. Foreign policy as conducted between states accepting roughly the same principles is an art of negotiation and adjustment. Foreign policy between different political cultures is a totally different matter. They may not (as in the case of the Soviet Union and the West) even take the same view about the meaning of negotiation. One of the errors of Western diplomacy is that those who direct it sometimes try to apply the principles of the first type of foreign policy to the second.

Some years ago the Foreign Office was faced with the

problem of getting the Russians to release Mr. Gerald Brooke, the London lecturer who had taken some 'anti-Soviet' literature into the USSR and been sentenced to a labour camp. Unlike President Kennedy, who secured the release of Professor Barghoorn after a couple of weeks by using every possible pressure, and unlike General De Gaulle who secured the exit of Michel Tatu's Russian wife and even his Russian stepchild by threatening to expel the Soviet ambassador, the Foreign Office behaved in the most abject fashion. Against the wishes of Brooke's colleagues, Soviet teachers on exchange visits were even allowed to come over to work at his own Polytechnic. I conducted something of a campaign in the press and on the radio, urging firmer measures, for it is the unanimous advice of Soviet dissidents that the maximum public uproar in the West is most effective in such cases. After some years when Brooke was finally let out he told me that I had been absolutely right; his wife, who had remained in England, had also agreed with me. But at the time, when I had argued with officials in the Foreign Office, I was always being told that Soviet officials had assured them quiet and patient negotiations would produce results so long as no public fuss was made and no one rocked the boat. The prevalent view in the Foreign Office was that 'diplomacy' was an all-purpose panacea, and that other methods were scarcely to be thought of. It is natural enough that professional diplomats often have a tendency to exaggerate the role of their own forte of negotiation even when negotiation is inappropriate (just as, since they are knowledgeable as to detail, they may not see the wood for the trees). The political leader must overcome this and use the diplomatic machine to implement definite policy.

Again, a prominent official of the State Department once told me, during the Kissinger period, that by quiet pressure and negotiation and the avoidance of public confrontation, the American government had secured the emigration of several important dissidents. But this is to submit to a hostage system. A great power cannot conduct its relations with another on the basis of a handful of individual cases, when a principle is at stake. If by releasing a dozen or so dissidents the Soviet government can silence much Western criticism which might have led to reductions in technological assistance, at the same time sending other dissidents off to labour camps and psychiatric hospitals without much public fuss, no more has been achieved than the payment of individual ransoms.

In the same way it would not have been correct for the Foreign Secretary to go personally to see President Amin to intervene for a British prisoner. Otherwise all foreign policy might begin to be conducted on the hostage principle. (And, apart from other disadvantages, there would be no time for anything else). Of course, there may be occasions in which a particular figure or a particular trial can be regarded as a test-case, and made the centre of public attention; but the person concerned is then taken as representative of a matter of principle, a precedent, and the negotiations are not simply on his behalf.

There is a tendency not only among diplomats to think that negotiation in itself is always a good thing. And this applies to the key matter of negotiation with the USSR and also to lesser issues. It should be obvious that there are times when inaction is preferable to action. Moreover, this attitude also leads to the idea that anything is negotiable. On the contrary, it is often the case that the best tactics are to declare a position to be absolutely non-negotiable. Having handed over half the world to the local inhabitants, we found ourselves faced with demands to cede territories like Gibraltar and the Falkland Islands where the inhabitants vigorously and almost unanimously opposed such cession. And now—in one of the few situations in which the United Nations actually supports our interests—the Government is hawking pieces of Belize territory without permission from the inhabitants. Once it has been conceded that our positions are negotiable in such cases, much of the harm is done, and it is very hard to reverse. In Belize, since the in-habitants seek independence, and will thus have the good fortune not to depend wholly on the will power of the British govern-ment, the situation may be retrieved—though even there the appetite of Guatemala has been sharpened. But in the cases of Gibraltar and the Falkland Islands it may be more difficult to return to a firmer position.

Professional diplomats (particularly since no longer a com-paratively small group with broader political education and more closely associated with real politics) have also to a certain extent succumbed to one of those tendencies inherent in their situation, that of finding a common interest with the amorphous mass of the world diplomatic establishment. That is, they begin to judge and to act less from the interests of their own country and culture and more from vocational solidarity. Moreover, they tend to judge the success of policies by the immediate effects in their own narrow sphere; for example, in some ephemeral vote in the United Nations. This *déformation professionelle* tends to divert them from the maintenance of their country's principles and power simply to gain a measure of support on individual points. They find it difficult to realise that a firm and forthright attitude may in the long run serve to rally rather than repel support, even if it results an adverse UN vote on the immediate issue.

When it comes to Third World attacks on the West for colonialism or neo-colonialism, the Western tactic has been to ignore them on the grounds that the Third World attitude in these matters is largely symbolical and rhetorical, and that words can never hurt us. Not only does the most extravagant abuse go unanswered, but also such disgraceful activities as a 'non-aligned' conference which gave unconditional support to North Korea. Of course it was originally true that much Third World abuse of the West was ritualistic, but this abject calculation fails to comprehend that to surrender the symbol is also to surrender the substance.

This almost unconscious professional tendency tends to affect or distort policy while appearing to implement it. The Foreign Office and its officials are usually amenable to political control, but such control must be enforced firmly and consciously, to prevent these built-in tendencies to wander. This is not to say that Foreign Office factions which favour a policy rejected by the Government may not argue the point. It is mainly a question of firm and vigilant political leadership in London. There are always reasons for doing nothing to implement a given decision or principle, at least for the present. Some of the reasons are sound, others not. It is the job of the political leader to select and decide.

To say that principles should be stated clearly and defended when necessary is not, as is sometimes argued, to suggest crudeness in tactics, or in the analysis of problems. It is not a question of black and white simplifications but neither is it true to say that everything is more or less the same shade of grey. It is simply a return to the true balance between principles and long-term interests on the one hand and the detailed conduct of foreign policy on the other.

In the United Nations, which could and should be a forum for our principles, things have changed since the time when I helped draft Barbara Castle's spirited counter-attacks on Soviet imperialism. Now we fail to answer back, never defend our views and work on the principle that fawning is the way to gain influence. This is a gross miscalculation, as was shown during Senator Daniel P. Moynihan's tenure as United States representative to the United Nations. Moynihan's style can be criticized in certain minor respects. It gave the public impression of being rather rougher than was entirely suitable, and this gave an opening to his critics (particularly in some of the speeches he made outside the UN). Nevertheless, in principle, his conduct was sound. He refused to tolerate the conventional anti-American outbursts of Third World representatives, and forthrightly maintained American principles. He answered the attacks of the Communist bloc, which had so often been allowed to go by default, with devasting counterattacks. His insistence on the right of America to have its interests and its ideals taken into account was extremely popular in the United States itself.

There were few Western voices in support of Moynihan. The British representative, Mr. Ivor Richard, went out of his way to insult our ally, as he had never insulted our enemies, with snide talk of cowboy tactics. Richard not only made no attempt to defend Western libertarian principles but even described them as merely a 'particular brand of political theology'. With inane piety he referred to the General Assembly as a 'democratic institution'—whereas, of course, it is (in Solzhenitsyn's words) not a United Nations at all but merely United Governments, the great majority elected by no one.

A number of the representatives of former colonial territories have no legitimacy except their claim to have led the anti-imperialist struggle. As Conor Cruse O'Brien has pointed out (in the *New York Review of Books* 16.9.76), in many cases the struggle which brought subsequent regimes to power was not to get rid of the British, who were leaving anyway, but to seize control of the new State from a variety of indigenous rivals. In this sphere, the West has accepted the terminology of its enemies, sometimes by default, but sometimes with active collaboration. 'National liberation' is freely used to describe movements whose aim is to impose their own gang rule.

Dr. Moynihan pointed out in a formal letter to the Secretary of State that although it had been alleged that his tactics would lose African and other Third World votes for American proposals in the United Nations, in the event the US had done rather better than usual whether as a result of his style or not: adequate refutation of a mere *a priori* assumption.

I chanced to be present at a 'colloquium' at the Smithsonian Institution in Washington at the time of the furore over Moynihan. The Italian Ambassador to the United Nations was the speaker, and he developed the patronizing and hostile view currently taken about Dr. Moynihan by various Western Europeans. Feeling that it was easier for myself than for Americans present to come to Moynihan's defence I put his case very strongly and argued that the Third World countries would in the long run prefer to be treated frankly as adults. Among those present was a distinguished Nepalese, himself a former ambassador to the UN, who spoke in support of my arguments.

I must make it clear that I am not urging tough or abusive attitudes. To be clear and forthright does not mean to attack, quarrel with, or impugn the motives of those who may disagree with us on given issues but not necessarily in principle or in the long run.

We should also establish a more critical and useful attitude to the UN agencies, in which a political struggle is waged by the Soviet Union and others, and is seldom countered.

A number of criticisms were made of the American withdrawal from the International Labour Organization in 1977. These were mainly to the effect that certain valuable sources of international cooperation would be lost. One may doubt whether these were proportionate to the funds paid (largely by the United States) to support a tax-free bureaucracy or to the failure by totalitarian regimes to implement 'ILO' policies. But the issue of principle was overwhelming. It has always been ridiculous that the representation of democratic countries in the ILO should be three-fold of government, employers, and trade unions—while these three elements in the Communist states are all represented by government men. There are no trade unions, merely bodies called trade unions, in the USSR and in a number of other countries. There is no reason why the countries which provide most of the money should accept this hypocritical arrangement. But when the 'majority' decided to use the organization for political aims directly opposed to those of West it was time and time to go. Britain should too. If the West cannot use such sanctions, or is not expected to do so, all similar organizations will turn against us. It is not only right for us to leave the ILO; it will be useful lesson to other international organizations.

Similar considerations apply elsewhere. It is not enough to say that an organization produces some good results, if it is at the same time grossly over-staffed. We should be as concerned with the waste of our money by an international bureaucracy as much as by an internal one: a committee of the House of Commons should watch our interests in these fields as vigilantly as any other expenditure of the taxpayer's money. We should stop our contribution to the funds of organizations which, in addition to their legitimate activities, are also being paid for activities harmful to the West—as, for example, with some of the commitments of UNESCO. Meanwhile, if the salaries of these international bureaucrats are to be untaxed, they should be markedly reduced to a scale matching the true value of their recipients.

On the other hand (for example) the United Nations Industrial Development Organization has been very successful, particularly in encouraging, and giving technical assistance to, free trade zones.

To sum up: the ways in which our representatives at the United Nations and elsewhere have failed to reply to accusations of imperialist excesses past and present does no good at all. We must not only rebut specific charges, but expose the real imperialism of the USSR. We should assert emphatically, on every occasion when the canard is raised, that there is no exploitation in good trade and other relations with underdeveloped countries, and that our own comparative wealth is not responsible for their poverty.

There is no reason, either, why we should accept misrepresentations about our conduct in the past. No doubt, it is understandable that nationalist politicians in the former colonies should represent their own history in terms of a struggle by local angels against foreign devils. It may even be natural, for those seeking an easy scapegoat, to blame all their present troubles on the colonial powers. But there is no reason why we should go along with this. It is a situation in which the political forces of such countries are automatically aligned against us, at the same time making demands on us.

Although we may agree that the ex-colonial peoples had to rule themselves eventually, (a position taken by our spokesmen from Macaulay to Kipling), this does not mean that we need accept the idea of a criminal imperial past. There were blemishes on our system of rule as with any other. But it can be easily shown that the benefits brought to the quarter of the world ruled by the old Empire—with fewer armed men, as Orwell points out, than were thought necessary by a minor Balkan state—far exceeded any harm.

It would be pleasant (and popular) for the British to hear their UN representatives firmly defending this and every other aspect of their system. Moreover, it would only be resented by the most mean-spirited demagogues of the new nations, and we can be reasonably sure that any publicly expressed offence will be more than matched by respect for those who defend their own. Controversy with our friends, or potential friends, can be conducted in perfect amenity without sacrificing the substance of our own point of view.

There are of course occasions when a problem is so complex or refractory that no clearcut policy is evident. In such circumstances, piecemeal negotiations and diplomacy in the hope of a step-by-step improvement, are the best tactics. Even in the sphere of Western-Soviet relations there are occasions for concessions, provided that these are made on both sides, and that they do not affect the substance of our position. One cannot object to minor inconsistencies, and it is often appropriate to seek improvements in a siatuation rather than complete solutions: but the improvements must be real, and tend towards the fuller solution.

The danger in negotiations of this sort is that supposedly 'practical' or 'pragmatic' men may urge the short-term benefits of vairous moves which on a longer view may harm the Western

position. They are the sort of people who were particularly
keen on trade with Germany in 1939, the men of whom Lenin
was thinking when he said that the bourgeoisie would sell the
Communists the rope they needed to hang them with.

As Dean Acheson remarked of Truman, he had learned

> the limits of international organization and agreement as means
> of decision and security in a deeply divided world. Released from
> acceptance of a dogma that builders and wreckers of a new
> world order could and should work happily and successfully
> together, he was free to combine our power and coordinate our
> action with those who did have a common purpose.

There is no need to bring heavy pressures to bear on the
Kremlin or to give them the impression that they have no choice
but a desperate throw against the West. But if the USSR is to
evolve into a peaceable member of the world community it
can only be as the result of being deprived of the rewards of
expansionism and turned back onto the problems of its internal
development. And for this, positive inducements from the West
are available—economic, technological and other aid given
precisely in proportion to Soviet psychological disarmament,
and not (as at present) without any quid pro quo. Political will
power, expressed in sensible policies, is what is needed.

The maintenance of our interests and our principles is not
simple and straightforward. If we were to act purely on the basis
of Right then we must demand the immediate withdrawal of the
Russians from (for example) the Baltic States. Reasonable
expediency and a view of the political possibilities of the
moment, must lead us to compromise in practice. There is
no reason for us to give up the principle, and we can hope
and work for it in the long run. For the moment there are good
arguments against pressing these matters as immediate demands,
but we should still raise the issues and keep them alive, particularly when retorting to ill-founded attacks on the 'imperialism'
of the West.

When we speak of our 'interests' let us insist that the economic
aspect of foreign policy is secondary and ancillary to more
general political considerations. A sacrifice of trade benefits
is nothing compared with the sacrifice of life itself. This would
seem obvious, but the recent 'think tank' report on the British

Foreign Office and Diplomatic Service openly took the view that economics should now be the essential theme of foreign policy, and this in a world where politics determines events to an unprecedented degree.

To urge a clear view of our interests and principles, and a firm understanding of the basic hostility of those who oppose our culture, is not to urge crudity in the diplomacy. These regimes exist, and we are required to negotiate with them. Ambassador Kohler tells us that the principles the US Embassy in Moscow followed in negotiation in his time were to be 'firm, patient, persistent, polite'.

We may summarize the general principles on which such negotiations should be based as follows:

(a) we should understand motives and propagate that understanding;

(b) while seeking all means of genuine cooperation with the USSR, we should insist on reciprocity. At present, we should accept their view of detente as a 'means of struggle' and counter any moves where they occur, or in other areas where we can act to their disadvantage;

(c) we should use persuasion and pressure to see that American-Soviet discussions on nuclear arms are not detached from the defence of the West as a whole, but closely integrated into it;

(d) we should work for a unified Western policy to deny the Russians the fruits of expansion in Africa and elsewhere outside the NATO area, as well as within it;

(e) we should seek to raise detente into a general and genuine system of peaceable relations by demanding, in return for any benefits we give the USSR, some measure of psychological disarmament.

A balance is needed in every field, internal and external, and that balance has everywhere been strained in recent years by one-sided theorists. In children's upbringing discipline *and* love are needed; in social policy, order *and* progress; in civic policy, law *and* liberty;—and in foreign policy, armed strength *and* peaceful intentions.

7

The Western Alliance

The unity of the West is vital if we are to match the unity of purpose of the Soviet programmes of armament and expansion. The Western alliance, in spite of some renewed vitality, is in serious trouble.

First, the negotiations on nuclear armaments between the USA and the USSR have been bilateral, and the other NATO nations have been given no effective voice. This is an intolerable situation, because any uncoupling of the question of nuclear arms from that of conventional arms at present leaves the US and the USSR with at the best nuclear parity, while in Europe a great superiority of Warsaw Pact conventional armament faces the armies, fleets and air forces of the NATO alliance.

At the same time, since NATO is by definition only concerned with the defence of one area of the globe, it does not present a united policy towards, for example, the Soviet initiatives in Africa. The present attitude seems to be that if the United States undertakes no serious action, the other Western powers feel that they cannot interfere. The one exception, and a most instructive one, was the French-Moroccan action in Zaire.

The questions of NATO and the EEC must be considered primarily from two aspects: first, the immediate defence of our culture against the USSR and its agents; and second, the development of a Western unity which could in the long run serve as a nucleus for development towards a democratic world order.

Alliances between free nations are always liable to strains and stresses; in a crisis the defence of the homeland becomes paramount, even at the cost of abandoning mutual solidarity. We can still learn from the story of Themistocles' desperate and barely successful efforts to keep the Greek fleet concentrated before the battle of Salamis, when half of its contingents had virtually decided to retreat into Fortress Peleponnese, which would anyway have been indefensible in the circumstances.

Britain, like the rest of the non-communist world, is in effect defended by the power of the United States. This puts an unfair burden on the Americans. On the other hand, it seems that the USA can commit us to certain policies which we have not directly helped to frame. Of course, alliances such as NATO mean that non-American states have reasonable rights of consultation and the ability to influence many decisions, and it is true that the Americans have since the 1940s pursued policies and treaties under which the defence of Europe is in principle treated as integral to their own. But their commitment has occasionally been a little shaky and American voices for withdrawal have sometimes been heard. When sensible Americans like John T. Roche start suggesting that the United States might withdraw within its continental limits, things have gone dangerously far.

It is equally possible to imagine a direct Soviet-American confrontation over some issue outside the direct purview of NATO—Israel, say, or Cuba. We could then be committed without an adequate say. Similarly, American decisions on armaments might leave—may already have left—NATO's European combat forces in a position of weakness for which they are not compensated by an adequate American nuclear credibility; once again we would be facing a crisis because of decisions over which we had had little control. All in all, we have a certain right to the cry 'No confrontation without representation'.

As by far the most powerful member of the Western alliance, the United States is bound to have a preponderant influence on the alliance's policies. In practical terms, it might not matter if only American decisions prevailed, so long as these were widely accepted as suitable. In recent years, however, there have been successive currents of policy which have aroused considerable disquiet among America's allies—and, indeed, among important sections of political thought within the United States. First, there was the confusion of aims emerging in the latest stages of the policy called 'detente'. This was not intended by its original framers, who wished to argue from strength, and to meet and rebuff Soviet aggression. As I have argued, that did not work owing to a failure to understand that Soviet Union is not an adversary similar to those within the old Concert of Europe, and a failure to appreciate that in America and the West it is no good telling the public at length that we are now on good terms with the USSR, and then expecting it suddenly to raise the willpower and vigilance to intervene in a crisis like Angola. The second, and present set of qualms arises from a fear that elements within the American administration believe that an arms agreement favourable to the USSR will defuse the situation rather than, as many of us would argue, make it more dangerous.

The United States may be still going through the last of the series of shocks which so severely shook its internal and foreign attitudes a few years ago. Until these temblors die down, a certain lack of commitment and consistency is apparent, particularly in foreign policy initiatives. On the other hand, the American public is clearly recovering its nerve. On the Panama issue, it was most encouraging to see the mood of a majority of Americans against any further cession of American interest, even if, for once, other people's interests might suffer. It is quite clear that the Treaty defends the remaining American interest in the Canal to a degree which would not have been politically possible but for the force of American public opinion.

The ancient Greeks found out that one disadvantage of the critical mind is that those who study, criticize, compare and generally bring their consciousness to bear on long-term policy are likely to be fulltime philosophers or academics, rather than practicing politicians. And their work—much more in modern times than in the ancient world—tends to keep them away from harsh reality, in favour of the clean white paper and the verbal models on their desks.

The present American tendency to appoint professors to positions of importance in the handling of foreign policy has a number of disadvantages, in this context. One is that they have not usually had to take real responsibility for failures, and have become opinionated and over-confident in their schemes. The wish to shine by propounding and attempting to put into effect some brilliant novelty, may detract from the need for soundness and good sense, which are essential to an adult foreign policy.

The disasters into which America was led in the 1960s stemmed largely from excessive academic self-confidence in the military and political spheres. (And it is not surprising that the one area of British policy for which academics were largely responsible was—the economy!)

As I write a number of qualms are being expressed in the United States about the conduct of foreign policy. Some of these are also the legitimate concern of any loyal ally. And in some cases it could be urged that America's allies should surely have been consulted. Indeed there is a strong argument in favour of foreign policy being much more carefully coordinated between the United States and her allies in both Europe and Asia.

The chief concern of the Asian allies is the proposal eventually to withdraw ground troops from South Korea. For the Japanese, any change in the area is clearly a matter of vital concern and other allies might query the proposal on the following grounds:

First, that the present arrangements have kept the peace for a quarter of a century, and there would need to be positive arguments in favour of any change.

Second, the North Korean government is one of the most aggressive states in the entire world and should not be encouraged lightly; (incidentally we have some right to be heard in this matter as British forces took part in repelling the earlier aggression).

Third, the argument that air support would be sufficient must rouse a certain uneasiness among those other states where American troops are stationed. For basically, the argument is not a military one at all. If your troops are on the ground you are automatically involved. If they are not, a political decision is required to provide the air support, and this decision may be negative. Above all, the fear must arise that this apparently pointless withdrawal is not the product of strategic thinking, but of an ideological undertow of isolation or appeasement.

There have been a number of similar examples in US foreign policy. A very minor one was the return of the Crown of St. Stephen to Hungary. For the question must instantly arise: what did America get in return? The answer seems to be, some expressions of goodwill from Hungarian Communist leaders. Curiously enough, the USSR made a similar symbolic gesture to pre-Communist Hungary in 1940, when the banners captured by the Tsarist armies in putting down the Hungarian Revolution of 1849–49 were returned to Budapest: but the Russians exacted a quid pro quo—the release and dispatch to the Soviet Union of the Hungarian Communist leader, Matyas Rakosi. If the Crown had been sent to the Government which had removed the representation of that crown from the Hungarian flag as soon as it came to power, in return for a general amnesty for political prisoners, that would have made some sense. Pleasant expressions on the faces of the Hungarian government do not amount to much. They are unable to do anything without the permission of the Soviet occupying power, as was shown by their abject participation in the crushing of Czechoslovakia in 1968. In a broader context, the return of the crown can be seen as a gesture of legitimization. For not long afterwards we had the American President's speech in Warsaw in which he made a number of remarks whose general effect was to legitimize the Gierek government.

It takes a considerable effort for Americans to feel the dangers which are so real in Europe. Soon after the invasion of Czechoslovakia in 1968, I was briefly in California. An Englishman, a professor at a major university, told me at some length of his uncomprehending horror at the shallowness of the reactions to the Russian assault and the absence of shock which he found among his colleagues. They shared the view that it was a dreadful and dangerous act. But the power of the feeling roused in Western Europe was missing.

I noticed this myself and not only in California. It was, surely, the effect of distance, and of the feeling of safety that it has historically induced. In England, the enemy has always been no more than a few hours away. Radar beacons now loom above the beaches where, in 1940, many of us were dug in, like others before us, back to the times of the Count of the Saxon Shore (one of whose units had been stationed only a few miles from my battalion's position).

This physical and imaginative distancing of the Americans from the marches of the democratic world is natural enough, and not a matter for blame. On the contrary, the country's political leaders' continued firmness on the European commitment is much to America's credit. So is the fact that, even in the aftermath of Vietnam, the majority of American public opinion still held that the United Kingdom—though admittedly no other overseas country—should be defended by American troops. This is perhaps the point at which one should assert firmly that the 'special relationship' still persists at the most profound level in the minds of the peoples of both the United States and Britain. There is nothing similar in our relations with the Western European countries, in spite of much recent talk. This deep mutual feeling, though not always readily translatable into political terms, must be taken into account in all our relations. It gives us more influence, and leaves us more responsibility in the alliance.

The seventies have seen a considerable withdrawal from the American attitudes of what is sometimes called the 'imperial' period at the beginning of the sixties. The United States no longer believes that it can solve all problems on its own. Indeed, in some circles the reaction has gone so far that there are now voices arguing that America can solve no problems at all; or that it does not matter if she cannot; or even that no problems really exist . . . On the other hand the United States remains conscious of its relative power, and is still sometimes inclined to solutions formulated entirely in Washington. We must hope for a gradual settling down into a more stable mode, with the opposite tendencies of unilateral decisions and unilateral surrender losing their force.

The United Kingdom has a vital role to play within the Western Alliance; we must press our point of view and insist on participation in all major moves. The American administration is hampered by appeasers in its lower echelons and among the US establishment, and can only be helped by our firmness. As the US provides such a high proportion of the power of the West, its decisions tend to be unilateral. Our recourse is two-fold. First, firmness of the type (though with a different aim) which gave De Gaulle such influence when France was very weak. Second, gaining the right to lecture the alliance by making adequate contribution to it—including, perhaps, assistance in the area we have absurdly abdicated east of Suez. We cannot claim that the USA has no ground for complaint against Europe. The American airlift of arms to Israel at the time of the Yom Kippur War could find no staging posts in Europe, except in Portugal. Then it was a question of matching a massive Soviet airlift from a longer distance and into a single airfield, and it might well have been disastrous. But for an immense superiority in American logistics, we might have been in a situation in which Western Europe looked to the United States to take necessary action, while itself refusing to help in any way. And this may yet lead to real trouble in similar circumstances, for Soviet airlift capabilities have vastly improved, as could be seen in the Ethiopian-Somali War.

Then again, the natural anxieties of the larger European members of the Alliance have led to a concentration on the 'Central Front' of the continent, with a comparative neglect of NATO's flanks. The British programme for weakening the southern flank still further, with the actual or projected abandonment of our bases in Malta and Cyprus, is a legitimate cause for complaint by the Americans and all others who take the larger view. This is part of a more general cheese-paring which involves also withdrawal from valuable posts outside the NATO area, such as the Maldives. Yet this type of base is worth far more in proportion than the same investment deployed elsewhere. And we must coordinate policy on such issues.

If sound foreign policy involves great attention to the springs of public will at home, it is equally true that the British government must concern itself with the morale of the Western alliance as a whole. In this case it is not usually possible to appeal directly to public opinion in the other countries of the alliance, but only by implication. Weakness in the conduct of foreign affairs—in particular vis-à-vis the USSR—is sometimes the product of vacillation or misunderstanding on the part of elements within an Allied government rather than among its subjects. To some degree, this may be true of the situation in the United States. The role of the British government should be to present its own views publicly and forthrightly. In negotiation with the United States, it should insist on the right to have such views taken into account in any decisions affecting the alliance as a whole, thus holding before the American government and the American people a clear and persuasive position.

We may criticize particular American attitudes: but we do so only because we regard our two societies as aspects of a single culture. The intimacy of our relationship makes it possible to be nearly as uninhibited in criticizing America's errors as our own. If I sometimes suggest a firm British stand against what appear to be American errors, a similar position is taken by many Americans: nor, of course, can we complain of much legitimate American criticism of our own position.

Far from dividing us, thrashing out our disagreements should unite us yet more strongly. The formulation of tactics in our relations with the United States when we may feel that Washington is perhaps in dangerous error needs considerable care. Naturally, the normal recourse will be to persuasion and all the gentler pressures and adjustments which may be feasible. But in really crucial matters we must reserve the right of positive disagreement, and sometimes even express it publicly. Without that option, and the knowledge that it might be used, our other modes of influence lose much of their power.

But the main point remains: such disagreements are the disputes of a single great culture which is at present fragmented. Our relationship with the USA is central.

Both the great parties in Britain, while supporting membership of the Common Market, are now in a pragmatic mood about the economic advantages, and sceptical of the original 'federal' notion of political unity in any tighter sense. The British public is largely disenchanted, too.

Meanwhile the whole étatiste and administrative conception of a modern economic order has lost the intellectual battle. It has only a residual momentum among that part of the political class which still maintains that the further intrusion of the state is plausible. Thus, both the more modern theorists on the one hand, and the mass of the population on the other, have had enough of bureaucratic solutions which solve nothing. The EEC owes part of its unpopularity in the United Kingdom to its bureaucracy and its obsession with regulations. The role of a sensible British leadership must be to fight against these tendencies within the EEC, as at home.

The proposed political unity of 'Europe'—i.e. a number, though not all, of the countries of Western Europe—is a heart-warming idea. Like so many heart-warming ideas—including, for example, the League of Nations—it is not founded in the realities of political and cultural tradition. It underestimates the national principle, or at least implies that it could be transcended by goodwill or administrative decision, and that France, Britian, Germany and Italy could without serious delay, or destructive crisis, become a political unity on a democratic basis. When we consider how people with far less to divide them, such as the Flemings and the Walloons or the Serbs and the Croats, are in a constant state of friction, part of the fallacy is exposed. When we consider how long it takes to establish a political tradition, the differences in this field alone between Britain, Denmark, Holland on the one hand, and such countries as Germany and Italy (and even France) on the other hand, our scepticism increases. The fact that in Germany and Italy democracy has more or less flourished for one generation does not seem adequate on a longer view; and we cannot forget that France was reduced to the verge of civil war on two occasions in the sixties. Now that we are in the EEC, we must work for the best. But even without further federalization, and regardless of the views of men of goodwill, the historical likelihood that everything will go smoothly, and that a further generation will pass without internal crisis, seems slight.

Part of the argument for British entry was precisely that the stability of British institutions and traditions would help to solidify the whole structure. We must hope that such a contribution will be effective, though in practical terms one can scarcely envisage it going so far as the form of British troops being used to put down an Italian Communist revolution (and one may equally feel that Continental troops are unlikely to appear in London to prevent a British secession). This is one of those matters on which a final judgement is impossible. The argument, *mutatis mutandis*, resembles the one about whether Britain in 1940 should have committed her entire air force to the defence of France. If it would have saved France, yes. If France had fallen all the same and Britian thereby left defenceless, no. It is generally believed that the decision taken was actually the right one.

If Britain is after all pushed into a tighter and more political union with the rest of Europe, it seems all the more certain that the bonds will chafe, and that a revulsion of feeling will leave us further from Europe than ever.

Many supporters of the Common Market see it as a step to a greater unity of the democratic culture which in no way excludes a further and later step which would unite 'Europe' with America, Australasia and Japan. On the other side, to objectors the Common Market appears a distorting and unnecessary detour: to be, at present *divisive* of the European culture—which is not geographically limited, but includes the Europes overseas. Above all we must avoid a smug allegiance to 'Little Europe' as opposed to the greater and more necessary unity of the democratic culture as a whole. We should already be thinking, however tentatively, in terms of a larger confederation.

The argument that a European 'Third Force' is useful or necessary does not seem to stand up very well to the question of what its precise object and role are supposed to be. Economically, such a Europe would be very rich—richer, in fact, than the whole Soviet bloc. Militarily, it is difficult to see that it would be any more effective than it is at present. If America were to become isolationist, we would have to do our best; the prospects would not be encouraging.

Russia is militarily powerful because the state is in a position to divert a far larger proportion of its wealth from consumer goods into armaments. America is powerful because it is so very wealthy. Democratic Europe would neither have the excess wealth of America, nor the possibility of squeezing the citizen like Russia. There are other perspectives (see Chapter IV) but they would be poor substitutes for the American alliance.

The closer political links within the Community, existing or proposed, do not constitute the only barrier against the USA, (and Canada, Australia and New Zealand too, to name a few). The *economic* arrangements themselves tend to increase such divisions, as the late Senator Humphrey once warned us. Britian should use whatever influence it has in the Community to amend its tendencies to 'Third Force' anti-Americanism and to economic autarky; as Dennis Healey has said, our membership is only tolerable if we are, in this sense, America's 'Trojan Horse' in the EEC.

During the EEC's history there have been long periods when the military alliance between Britian, America and five of its members have been stronger than those linking the latter to

France. Therefore there seems no reason why Britain should not, at least militarily, be linked with the transatlantic and transpacific democracies at least as strongly as with its partners on the Continent. The Common Market arrangements do not exclude political unions with other states—just as (loose and unimpressive though they may be) the French Union and the Commonwealth subsist regardless of the Treaty of Rome. It seems unlikely that links such as those which exist between French African territories and the EEC would be suitable for our relations with the more powerful states beyond the ocean. Nevertheless some form of expansion of the EEC into a broader economic and political unity, in which the shakier democracies of the Continent would not play so dominating a role, may be feasible; we could work towards it. However, it seems that a greater unity is more likely to result from, at the lowest, some attenuation of the British links with the EEC, to match a greater enhancement of links with the USA and the others.

The true evolution should surely have been (and may yet be) towards, first of all, a grand confederation of the United States, United Kingdom, Canada, Australia, New Zealand, and the Caribbean and Pacific countries, and perhaps Norway, Denmark and the Netherlands. 'Europe' under the protection of this much larger entity, would have been in a stronger and more stable positions; and, would have been less likely to fall victim to 'third force' delusions, (which would have been less dangerous under these circumstances).

The objection to the more extreme version of the 'Europe' concept is that it cuts contrary to the historical grain; when President Pompidou announced that Britain must henceforth turn 'away from the open seas' he was falling into the shallow error of those who think that a culture can, in a short time, be forced into different channels by a political act.

This is not to denigrate the power of that more general tradition of civic cultures based on checks and balances, rather than autocratic decision, which exists in continental Europe; still less to deny the importance of encouraging and strengthening their potential, if this is done in the right way. But attempts to force changes on abstract grounds are counter-productive, and should be avoided in any suggested future arrangements. In particular, obsession with GNP statistics diverts attention from political and cultural problems into a narrow, and in the long run, indecisive field. It is this obsession which has led in 'Europe' to the development of an insensitive economic bureaucracy, an authoritarian element which is likely to backfire and throw the game to the disintegrative elements.

I would argue in favour of taking a long-term view of Britain's place in the Western alliance, stressing the importance of the political interests and trends of our culture, rather than the narrow economic considerations. An increase of a few percent in the GNP is little compensation for the distortions and pressures of a forced and unnatural political arrangement. The true path to Western unity should be a gentle progress towards a flexible confederation of countries of the same language, legal tradition, and general culture.

It may be felt that such a view has been overtaken by events. I would argue that this is not quite the case. In the first place, the United States and Britain should be prepared for the contingency of the collapse of Western European political unity. But, leaving that aside, and accepting the political and economic forms now in existence, we may still hope that the road to Western unity has been distorted, rather than an abolished. As a first step, then, we should work against those economic and other tendencies which divide the Common Market from the United States. This involves the lowering of American as well as European trade barriers; the economic obstacles which have been gratuitously built up must be reduced before any further advance to political union can take place. Despite the bureaucratic rigours of the EEC, there is no reason why Britian on her own or with like-minded countries, should not seek closer political relations with the US. General de Gaulle's France showed how a country, under similar treaty constraints within Europe, was nevertheless able to carry out a foreign policy independent of, and to some degree hostile to, those of the other members; and even to leave the North Atlantic Treaty Organization. Britain could carry out her obligations under the Treaty of Rome, (even though I for one would prefer to see that heavily amended), while at the same time moving independently in the opposite direction to that of Gaullism—towards a closer political relationship with the US and the other 'oceanic' countries; (most of the latter are, like

Europe and the United States, going through a period of disarray in their international conceptions). We could do this while at the same time working inside the EEC to break down the economic barriers against America.

The United States is nowadays less willing to undertake the enormously preponderant role in the West's foreign and military arrangements which has fallen to it since the war. Unity with other countries of the same tradition would both ease the American task and spread some of the American responsibility. Countries which have, however unintentionally, relied on the Americans, and have not had to face either the responsibilities or the decisions of world power, would be brought into the central processes. (We have seen such absurdities as the effective British withdrawal from the Indian Ocean, carried out on purely parochial grounds).

We need a more general unity of the countries with free constitutions. It has been remarked that truly modern economies, and modern democracies, are only to be found in those countries with traditions which were never entirely despotic; that Western Europe and Japan were the only cultures in which even 'feudalism' consisted of a system of mutual rights and obligations—that is, a genuine civic culture, as against those which have prevailed in Russia and in most of Asia. This is true even though some of those countries have nevertheless contained forces which at times imposed a despotic rule upon the sound foundations (in Japan, of course, as much as in Germany or Italy). The coming together of the Continental and Japanese cultures with those of Anglo-Saxon 'Oceania' should be a natural development in the near future, so long as forced and artificial political structures do not distort it. (We should also, of course, consider the position of Israel, and of countries such as Gambia, the Philippines and parts of South America.)

The basic principles of our culture were, indeed, covered by the original Atlantic Charter. The difficulty has been that the despotic regimes of the Communist bloc are willing to subscribe to the same form of words. A new charter would need to be drafted with considerable care, using a form of words to which supporters of our society can subscribe, and to which totalitarians cannot. The word 'democracy', in particular, must be used with the utmost discretion and be rigorously defined.

Resisting the temptation to draft such a charter, I would suggest that its main elements should be as follows:

    (a) a powerful propounding of the thesis of the open, pluralistic society;

    (b) an assertion that the successful solution of social and political problems is only reached by the free discussion of alternatives;

    (c) the practical possibility of replacing a government elected to forward one policy by another;

    (d) denunciation of the theory that a dictatorship, a planned economy and society, is more efficient or scientific;

    (e) a denunciation of the shallowness as well as the impracticality of utopianism.

Obviously today there are problems which were not envisaged in the forties; first those which may be described as environmental; and second those concerned with the underdeveloped countries. (We should be able to cut through most of the current cant about the latter and perhaps even persuade people that the provision of large-scale financial aid to these countries is sometimes not only unhelpful but counter-productive.) We need to make a new alignment and a conscious effort towards closer unity of the powers which are the bearers of civilization in our time. Such a dynamic development will be attractive to the countries of the intermediate or potentially democratic world, and also to the peoples of the closed despotic ideocracies which face us. The prospect of progress through Western unity to world unity is the only one which provides any real hope for our time.

The splendid idea of a united world, and of a reconciled humanity, is one of the aspirations which many are tempted to feel can be achieved by main force—world revolution—or by premature agreements which plaster over real rifts. A true perspective must surely see such unity as evolving gradually from a unity of the politically civilized portion of our planet.

8

Other Communisms

Another largely European problem will face us if communists enter the Government in Italy, or elsewhere among the membership of the Western alliance. Some argue that the Italian Communists, and others, have an allegiance to multi-party democracy, and completely repudiate the USSR and its ways. It is theoretically possible that a communist party could evolve into a democratic organization: (indeed it can be argued that the Hungarian Communist Party did just that in the brief days of Imre Nagy's ascendancy, but that was in very different circumstances). What has occurred to make us rely on the Italian, French or Spanish communists as trustworthy allies?

To read some commentaries, one would think that the main motive of Italian communists is opposition to the Soviet Union. This is to ignore the fact that they are, as their name implies, communists. Their main aim is the establishment of a communist regime, and on the world scale the overthrow of 'capitalism': that is, of the political and social order of the West. In doing so, it is quite plausible that they would prefer to avoid coming under direct Soviet control. They nevertheless accept the ideology of the Soviet Union in principle, with a few particular criticisms; while they reject the West in principle.

The Italian Communist party remains organized strictly on the principles of 'democratic centralism'; it is fully under the control of its central leaders. They have, indeed, to manoeuvre to keep their mass support, but this is not relevant to their long-term principles. They remain Leninists. Those who suggest that they have changed are asking us to believe that they have abandoned their most solidly established beliefs.

It is clear enough that no party is going to gain power in the West if it admits that it would behave just like the Soviet Communist Party. By now we all know too much about the USSR. On the other hand, all communist parties are entirely the product of—and remain openly devoted to—Leninism, the Soviet ideology. If they have changed into democratic socialists, why do they accept this theory of irreconcilable struggle to the end—supposedly between classes, but actually between communists and others. It cannot be too often repeated that the key Lenin phrase is 'Who-whom?': in all political circustances one side or the other will be crushed; there is no prospect whatever of genuine collaboration; all compromises and alliances with other parties are 'forms of struggle' against them; communists support socialists with a view to destroying them.

The other aspect of Leninism is the doctrine of the centralised party machine controlling the members. If a communist party had become democratized, its first natural move would be to dismantle this authoritarian structure. None has done so.

The Italian Communists are the most sophisticated practitioners of the new 'civilized' line—in public. Yet one Italian Communist Senator is quoted in the *New York Times* as saying openly that the multi-party system is no more than a 'transition stage'; another gives an interview to the Western press affirming that when it comes to the crunch his party will always be on the Soviet side; others impress observers as even being reconciled, if the worst comes to the worst, to serving as Soviet puppets. Nor can we just forget that the leaders are all men who, financed by Moscow through Prague, in their time unanimously accepted Soviet control, and even announced publicly in 1947 their party's readiness to welcome Soviet troops into Italy. Perhaps they have changed their minds. But we need something better than their assurances, and we also need an explanation of why they then happily remained loyal to a party which took such a stand.

We are now told that backward and barbaric Russia produced a backward and barbaric version of socialism, but that the Western European experience will transmute this to something truly democratic and amicable. This is nothing new. We were told in 1945, when the Czechoslovak Communists formed a coalition with the democratic parties, that these particular communists were brought up in a Western society, had parliamentary experience, would be different from the others. The difference, after 1948 when the mask slipped, was that they were if anything worse terrorists even than their other East European counterparts. Neither 'background' nor promises meant much.

So what are we to say to the promises of Western Europe's communists today? The first point, of course, is that they cannot come to power unless they make such promises. And similar promises were made by Lenin himself in 1917. He promised to respect the will of the democratically elected Constituent Assembly, but when it met he sent armed troops to suppress it. He promised freedom of the press, and all the other freedoms . . . he also advised communists to deceive where necessary.

It is clear that the Kremlin hates a situation in which any criticism of the USSR emerges in the Western communist parties. It intrigues to overthrow the local leaders (as it did with the Spanish party through its stooge, the Civil War General Lister); it actually split the Greek party. But more generally, the Soviet Politburo continues to recognize the Italian, French, British and other parties; it sends representatives to their congresses; it welcomes their delegates to Eastern Europe. It would like to control totally the Western European parties, but, so long as it cannot, it sees their uses in undermining the West as more than counterbalancing their marginal rudeness towards Moscow. Similarly, the Western parties would wish, if they came to power, to avoid domination by Russia; but their communist committment nevertheless aligns them primarily against the Western democratic order.

The fact that a communist party is wholly or partially independent of Moscow in no way guarantees a committment to democracy or tolerance. Communist Albania hates Moscow, but is itself the most virulent tyranny in Europe. Rumania, whose leaders Moscow continually plots to overthrow, is nonetheless one of the worst of the dictatorships of the Balkans. And the 'Euro-Communists', with the partial exception of the Spanish, are not independent even to that degree. They object to a number of specific Soviet actions, such as putting writers in strait-jackets and poisoning them with drugs. But they make it quite clear that if the Kremlin gave up these particularly repulsive policies they would have nothing in principle against the 'socialist' world of the USSR, whose errors amount to no more than a few excesses, but who essentially on the right lines.

A true evolution of communist parties into democracy would be one of the most hopeful developments we could seek, and it is no wonder that optimists try to make the most of any hopeful signs. The final abandonment of the Leninist notion of struggle to the death is desperately needed in the world today, for it is that murderous dogma which lies behind all our worst troubles, from the urban gunman to the threat of the hydrogen bomb. It may come about. But to take it on trust, on the assurance of people whose deepest convictions tend the other way, would be to let ourselves in for the horrible experiences of the Poles or Czechs, at best; at worst, it could undermine the will of the West, and lead to the collapse of our own political and military defence. Hence its attractions for some.

In Italy, in particular, the tactics seem to be: promise absolutely anything. The Communists there have already built up a new class in the cultural and administrative field, receiving much of the undeserved income which in communist states goes to the privileged bureaucracy. The party, having rotted the social order from inside, evidently hopes to take over without much extra trouble. Softly, softly, says the new communist monkey-stalker.

When a communist party has come to power (by what ever means) then held and lost free elections, and subsequently given up power—all the things we automatically demand of a civilized democratic party—then and only then might we feel some reassurance. But the Euro-Communists do not even go through the motions of urging free elections in Poland or East Germany. The Italian Communist attachment to freedom, has yet to provide the minimal evidence of, for example, telling the Russians that a social-democratic party should be legal in Czechoslovakia. Why don't they? If they did, there might be some slight reason for paying attention to their arguments. As it is, every consideration, and every clue, tells against trusting them. Even if there are communists who sincerely believe in reconciliation, the Leninist doctrine and party machine inevitably ensure that the real power is in the hands of the terror-bureaucrat, however much individual leaders may smile and smile.

It is sometimes argued that the Western powers should not express views about the coming to power of Italian communists, or openly discuss the changes of policy towards Italy which such an event would cause. The argument is that such utterances will cause ill-feeling among the Italian voters and will possibly impel them—at the price of cutting off their noses to spite their faces—to vote Communist when they might otherwise not do so. Similar objections have been made to the powerfully expressed views of the British Labour Party and the German Social Democratic Party on the question of socialist-communist alliances.

But why should not states and parties give their opinions? Surely it is only fair and reasonable that democratic states should point out that the coming to power of a government which is in principle hostile to them will effect their policies towards the country concerned.

It may prove impossible to keep communists out of the Italian Government. What Italy seems to need is a realignment of parties on the ruins of the worn-out Christian Democrats, as happened in Australia after the collapse of the United Australia Party, or in France recently, or many times in Greece. It may be too late. And we may soon have to face the problem and deal with it as best we can. But let us not be deluded, or make concessions in advance. It is sometimes argued that Iceland remained in NATO with communists in the government; but Iceland provided bases, not armies, and there was never any prospect of the communists overwhelming their self-confident coalition partners. In Italy I would expect communists in government to be very moderate at first, that Italian 'salami tactics' would slice very thin. The Czechoslovak Communists acted with apparent loyalty in that country's coalition government from 1946 till the unfortunate day in February 1948 when the mask, having done its job, was thrown aside.

It follows that we cannot accept communist membership of a NATO government in any real sense. If communists do, indeed, get into the French or Italian Governments, we would have to handle the situation as best we could—and in certain circumstances we can envisage a delicate relationship. But to behave as if the situation were as safe as ever would be to take enormous risks on the basis of a blind optimism.

We are sometimes told that if a country 'chooses' to go Communist in 'free elections', that is all right. But elections cannot be called 'free' if they are irreversible. Otherwise, we would have an absurd situation. A variety of parties could gain a majority in almost any country, if the electoral clock were stopped at the time chosen by themselves. People who talk that way would not think of accepting the following proposition: 'if the Conservatives win the next election, even by deceiving the electorate with false promises, then they are entitled to abolish the electoral system and remain in power for ever'.

It is not, of course, the case that any country has actually voted in a communist government in free elections. If one did, it would present us with various practical problems. But there would be no reason to accept its taking over as a democratic procedure, unless it had given credible guarantees that in four or five years the people would be allowed a free opportunity to confirm or reverse their decision. This seems particularly necessary, it might be added, in a party coming to power for the first time; in that case the voters must be relying absolutely on promises, and not at all on experience. Unless and until communist parties are reconciled with democratic civilization by accepting this simple ground rule of democracy, there is—in principle at least—no reason why they should be allowed to benefit from its customs.

Progress towards political civilization means a real willingness to accept that a non-communist regime, that non-communist ideas and non-communist parties, are legitimate, and that a genuine competition of ideas can take place. If free elections could be held under a prospective communist government, and that government replaced peacefully, there would be no democratic objection to a country choosing communism. If free elections were held in any currently communist country, then one could grant the right to the communists to win free elections in the outside world.

It seems fairly certain that, given six months of free organization Russia itself (and every other communist country) would at any time in the last sixty years have voted in a moderate Agrarian-Socialist coalition with a landslide. Since the forcible suppression of Russia's last freely elected body, the Constituent

Assembly, in 1918, 'the legislative powers, incapable of annihilation, have returned to the people at large'. The day they could exercise them would mark the end of the extreme international tensions of our time, as Engels remarked.

An idea behind some recent Western foreign policy moves seems to be that a line can be drawn in Europe between the Soviet and Western blocs, and that agreement, detente, and general stability in the area can be consolidated on that basis. There is, of course, a major fallacy in the notion that the Soviet Union would in any case regard a Western sphere as inviolable. It is argued that so long as Western power and morale on this side of the line are maintained, and all attempts to 'Finlandize' Western Europe resisted, a settlement of this sort would be advantageous, and such an 'Ostpolitik' could eventually lead to a more positive easing of tensions between states and between ideologies.

However, there is a hidden assumption here. Such a stability implies that Eastern Europe itself will remain reasonably calm. The opposite is true. Tensions within the Soviet bloc, far from easing, are becoming more and more dangerous. Whatever the attractions of avoiding war by dividing the world into Western and Russian spheres of influence, this scheme cannot be valid in the long run. Spheres of influence are only stable either if the states and peoples within a given sphere are content to be there, or if the great power concerned is in total military and political control. Clearly, since the fall of Stalin, the second of these conditions has not applied in Eastern Europe, while the first has never done so. Thus, successive political crises are inevitable in the whole of the East European section of the Soviet bloc. Already during the period of the Soviet domination seven out of the eight states in the region have rebelled in one way or another.

The American President's Warsaw message to the Polish people, (with remarks about the lack of oppression in that country, its praiseworthy relations with the USSR, and of his personal friendliness toward Gierek himself) seems to have been that the regime must be accepted. We seem to be back to the 'Sonnenfeldt Doctrine'. Yet whatever its abstract appeal, the notion of stable spheres of influence is fallacious on two grounds: first, there is no comparable policy on the Soviet side against destabilizing the governments of Western Europe; secondly, stability in Eastern Europe is a chimera: the governments have not struck roots, and their policies (especially in Poland) are such as to ensure further outbursts of the sort we have seen in one of another country every few years since the early 1950s. Needless to say, Western Europe has its own legitimate interests in developments in Eastern Europe, possibly more urgent and immediate than those of the United States; we should surely ask for a coordinated allied policy in such matters.

One notable recent change in the intellectual world of Eastern Europe is the virtual disappearance of the idea that a 'liberal communism' is possible. As Leszek Kolakowski has noted, these

> dreams about rejuvenated or regenerated communism, or even about Leninism that would not be Stalinism, the reveries which may now appear as intellectually pitiful, played their role in the disintegration of the system whose one weakness is its inability to do without an ideological facade which provides its principles of legitimacy. Precisely because it has drawn attention to the grotesque contrasts between the phraseological facade and the true realities of social life, the concept of a non-totalitarian communism, which to many of us today seems like the idea of fried snowballs, became one of the main factors in the present ideological disintegration of communism.

But, is now a dying idea . . . Then again, even between groups of repressive *apparatchiks*, the Rumanian leadership presents a problem which will require a great deal of flexibility on the Soviet side. It is not merely that the Rumanians are working to loosen and decentralize the military alliance. There have for some time been signs of a definite tendency to neutrality. Moreover, Ceaucescu has implicitly put the question of Bessarabia on the agenda: there is no doubt that, on the ethnographical principle which Moscow professes, all except the southern strip of this Soviet territory should go to Rumania. The attempts to proclaim a separate 'Moldavian' language, with a Cyrillic alphabet, have been derisory. But this is a sensitive matter in Moscow; Bessarabia (Brezhnev's old fief) is the only borderland of all those from which the Communist retreated in 1918–20, whose loss they never recognized in the years which followed.

Maps continued to appear showing it as rightfully Soviet. Moreover, as with the other troubles represented by Rumania, once
the principle is conceded, the remaining Soviet borderlands,
seized (as Chinese communists remark) from neighbouring
states, are at risk.

All in all, Eastern Europe remains a powder keg, and there is
no question of Western influence calming down these seces-
sionist and rebellious tendencies, and achieving stability on the
basis of the status quo. For the reasons are absolutely fundamental. The communist culture has simply not 'taken' in
Eastern Europe. Most of these nations have not undergone, or
have long since broken free of, the servile condition which the
Russians were forced to endure for 700 years. The demand for
personal and national liberty is ineradicable. These countries
are willing to live at peace with, and even in alliance with, the
Soviet Union, and to admit Russia's supremacy in the area as a
great power. If the Russian leadership would settle for that,
then—and only then—could a 'sphere of influence' policy be
viable. But they have not done so and show no signs of wishing
to do so. This is not an internal matter for the countries concerned, nor even for the Soviet bloc. It is a decisive factor for
peace or otherwise in Europe.

While it is true that Western governments sometimes express
a wish for a measure of liberty in Eastern Europe, our statesmen
do not press for it with the same militancy that the USSR uses
to extend its own system. Believers in detente tell us we should
not cause trouble in the area. But, again, the liberties of Eastern
Europe are primarily part of the human rights issue, which
remains our only substantial demand and bargaining counter in
negotiation.

In the present state of the world some form of alliance with
Communist China would be sensible, whether formal, or simply
factual. It is clearly in the West's interests that—for example—
military hardware should be made available to Peking.

It is true that in the very long run communism in its Chinese
form also represents a threat to the Western democratic culture.
But it does not do so now, partly because of a comparative lack

of power, and partly because of its far more serious and immediate hostility to the USSR.

In 1969, long before the Nixon-Kissinger opening to Peking,
I urged a Committee of the US Senate to approach Communist
China. But I warned that it was bound to lead to a certain
amount of enthusiasm among the lunatic fringe for a newly
respectable Peking regime. And, from ping-pong to acupuncture,
from the 'rehabilitation' of the old Yenan lobby to the raptures
of left-wing actresses, this has indeed come about. So long as
policy-makers and the sounder elements of public opinion are
not affected, this may be thought an unfortunate but unavoid-
able price that has to be paid.

However, this mood tends also to bring a euphoric urge to do
anything whatever to please Peking. It should hardly need
saying that the establishment of an alliance (or similar relationship) with China does not mean that we have to give them
everything they ask, or risk losing their co-operation. Since
there are plenty of voices in the West who urge that we should
make gratuitous and unilateral concessions to the USSR, an
opponent, for fear it might otherwise become even nastier, there
are bound to be those who feel that an ally, or a near ally, might
similarly abandon us unless we give into its every wish. This is
nonsense. Peking needs us as much as we need it, if not more so.
The idea that they might become hostile if the West does not
hand over Taiwan, for example, is chimerical.

Indeed, there are certain demands we can make of them.
At meetings of the Central Committee of the Chinese Communist Party in the early 1940s Mao Tse-tung adduced as a
model of tactics the 'Period of the Three Kingdoms'; Kingdom
A won because, while attacking Kingdom B in alliance with
Kingdom C, it simultaneously undermined Kingdom C. This
certainly resembles the Communists' conduct in their alliance
with Chiang Kai-shek against the Japanese. However, it should
clearly be a part of our policy towards the Chinese to press
them to renounce anti-Western activity in practice, if not in
theory; and to use their influence with various African and
other governments against the Soviet-Cuban interventions. At
present they seem to be pursuing this policy, to some extent,
and it is remarkable evidence of the intensity of their hostility
to the Soviet Union. In Sweden the most orthodox Maoist

group has called for a great rearmament to face Soviet aggression and similarly in Spain. Such was the view they took in Angola. Yet they continue to support Mugabe in Rhodesia . . .

In the nature of things the Western relationship with China is largely an American concern. Nevertheless, the Chinese themselves are particularly interested in the strength of NATO as a whole, and (partly to maintain their theoretical position of being against the 'hegemony' of the two great powers), they seek to establish stronger relations with a united Europe. So we may have a certain amount of leverage.

A co-ordinated Western policy should at least prevent us from further repetition of our split voting in the United Nations on the issue of seating Taiwan as well as mainland China. Naturally the exclusion of Taiwan was Peking's maximum aim, but there was no reason why the British Government's role should not have been persuasion and pressure, rather than surrender. This is not to deny the necessity of an effective alliance with Peking in present world circumstances. And there is much we can offer which the Chinese Communists want, both in arms and in the co-ordination of resistance to Moscow.

9

The Third World

It has become fashionable to say that the fundamental problem of international politics is the resolution of divergences between the richer and poorer countries—the 'north-south relationship'. This is sometimes treated as a source of potential antagonism, which might lead to a vast world Jacquerie.

It is clear that such a problem exists. Whether it is the major problem of foreign politics is more doubtful for two reasons: first, the desire for prosperity in the Third World will not be met by the moral Danegeld methods now largely accepted on both sides (and many Third World leaders have enough sense not to kill off the golden geese); and secondly any political and military threat from them is quite unreal except as a minor weight in the scales of the Soviet-Western conflict.

This is not to argue that relationships with the Third World are unimportant, particularly in the larger context of East-West relationships. We must return to sound principles in foreign policy in our relations with both groups. It has often been said that it is better to be hated than despised. But, generally speaking, those who hate us on principle are not a majority of the Third World. And those who now despise us, or who hate us only because they despise us, are more likely to side with a bulldog than with a jellyfish. Above all, we must discredit the notion that the USSR is free from the taint of imperialism, and is the legitimate ally and sponsor of all Third World claims and ambitions. Western countries are in a defensive position although they pay out, in aid to the Third World, sums greatly in excess of the trickle of Soviet alms.

It has long been the practice of Communist countries and the more 'militant' representatives of the Third World to attack the Western record, in the United Nations and before the world public in general, while representatives of the West do not answer back. This is an extraordinary change from attitudes in the fifties, when Labour and Conservative, Democrat and Republican alike freely counter-attacked the Soviet Union's hypocritical 'anti-imperialism' (and exposed internal horrors like the forced labour system). At present we appear to have accepted the following rules for behaviour in the UN and elsewhere on the international stage: (a) the West is to blame for the backwardness of the Third World; (b) the Third World should not be discouraged from setting up and maintaining regimes similar to that of the Soviet Union, (which are certain to prevent economic progress); (c) the West may not intervene against such counterproductive policies, even with advice, but must merely offset the inevitable failures by paying out large sums without any guarantee of political friendship in return; (d) the USSR has no imperialist record, is to be regarded as a natural support to the Third World, and is entitled to intervene, with mercenaries if necessary, to ensure the defeat of pro-Western elements.

Acceptance of these 'rules' gives the Russians an immense advantage, and a world reputation they in no way deserve.* In the Third World it encourages all those trends most hostile to the West, (and in the Western countries themselves it appeases those who hate their own culture, thus undermining the political will of the democracies from within).

The policy we should adopt is a firm rebuttal of anti-Western slanders, on every occasion, as a matter both of principle and of practical politics; and the equally forceful exposure of Soviet hypocrisy on the colonial issue, giving chapter and verse on the cases of Baltic States or Central Asia. Thus our own friends would be politically encouraged and ideologically armed, and the dupes or agents of the Kremlin thrown on to the defensive for a change.

The need for a return to sound principles in foreign policy applies equally to our relations with the Soviet bloc as it manifests itself in the Third World, and to the Third World in its own right. It is quite usual these days to have the issue of

---

* Both Brezhnev and his leading supporter Suslov have themselves served as colonial governors:— Brezhnev as Stalin's viceroy in Rumanian inhabited Moldavia, Suslov in Lithuania.

Puerto Rican liberation raised by a Third World-Communist grouping against the United States, but not that of Estonia against the USSR. Similarly the United Kingdom is regularly accused of vicious imperialism for retaining Gibraltar and the Falkland Islands, with no reference to, for example, Soviet Georgia. The free elections which invariably show these territories to be unwilling to give up their respective American or British connection are simply ignored, as is the fact that no true election takes place in the Soviet colonies. In the last Puerto Rican elections the independence parties gained five per cent of the vote on that island; but, on present form, that fact will not be emphasized by the USA at international meetings. Similarly, in spite of a determined British attempt to persuade the Gibraltarians to accept some arrangement with Spain, the voters there returned a huge majority for the status quo. In the case of the Falkland Islands, Argentina has admitted the British affiliations of the population, but has said flatly, with the support of the 'uncommitted' nations, that in this instance self-determination must be ignored. Britain has failed adequately to refute this argument before the 'uncommitted' nations who heard and subscribed to it.

I should make it clear that I am not necessarily urging attacks on Soviet colonialism at every possible opportunity, but merely that when we are wrongfully attacked we should counter-attack. The fact that, at present, *we do not even do that* speaks for itself. How often nowadays does one hear a Briton or a Frenchman praising his country's historical record in comparison with Soviet colonialism, or with the present condition of the former empire? This has been left to those like the spokesmen of the opposition parties in Mrs Ghandi's India who publicly pointed out the superior liberties they had enjoyed under the British Raj . . .

Another argument which has not been refuted adequately is the Leninist concept of the 'exploitative' nature of Western colonialism. In Lenin's (still orthodox) view, the whole point of imperialism was the export of capital to the backward countries where, owing to the low wage rates, 'super-profits' would be made. In no sense was this a true account of the economic development of the colonial territories. There was no great capital investment. In fact British investment abroad involved hardly any net outflow of capital. The French colonies imported more than they exported. And where there was major investment, it did not produces uper-profits; the Rand mines, for example, gave an average annual return of not more than 4.1 per cent.

There are other fallacies in the Marxist account of imperialism: for example, the incorrect assertion that 'finance capital', under the control of the great banks, supported colonial expansion. Yet the whole concept is now widely accepted, and anyone who points out that, for example, the trade balance between Britain and India was virtually unaffected by independence, or produces any other facts to spoil this over-simplified picture, is regarded as a dangerous eccentric. And, of course, it is worse still to draw attention to Russia's as yet unliberated colonies, and perhaps even quote Chekhov's remark (which is omitted from the Soviet edition of the *Collected Works*) that while both the Russians and the British had annexed foreign territory, the Russians had not given the inhabitants much in exchange, as the British had.

In all international bodies, we should proclaim the superiority of the Western political process; we should carry the argument to the Russians, denouncing their crimes and weaknesses; and we should politely convey the warning to the Third World that the West will not reward hostility towards itself.

Diplomatic problems are inevitable in relations with Africa and the rest of the Third World, though these are made more virulent locally and more dangerous on a world scale by the Soviet presence. It is absurd to argue that we can leave these vast, rich and heavily populated territories to the USSR and retreat to 'Fortress Democracy'—if only because a huge increase in Soviet material power and self-confident aggressiveness would inevitably ensue.

In these areas a dictatorship may occasionally be justifiable, or suitable for our support against a worse alternative. But we must never concede that a one-party state is *superior* to parliamentary democracy; rather that a backwardness which is excusable for local reasons may allow better things to emerge.

Before the war, and in the first post-war decade, it was generally assumed in the more backward parts of the world that political democracy was the most advanced form of the state. Countries which remained wholly or partly dictatorships nevertheless accepted that this was due to their temporary backwardness, and aspired in principle to a more democratic condition. Turkey was a prime example, as we saw with its constant intervention by the Army and its equally constant return to a limited degree of parliamentary democracy. But where Turkey was a model it is now an exception. The new dictatorships, military or otherwise, no longer apologize and urge their temporary nature. On the contrary, justifying themselves in Leninist jargon, they represent the one-party state as desirable in itself, and superior to 'bourgeois democracy'.

The Western democracies have made matters worse by failing to assert the superiority of their position in the international forums, in public speeches at home, and also in their direct relations with the Third World. In the first place, this encourages well-meaning Afro-Asians to drift towards 'one-party democracy' since they do not feel that anyone on our side will care one way or the other. They do not even hear an incisive exposure of the barbarian regressiveness of Marxism-Leninism. When they attack us we treat them like children with tantrums, allowing them to go on, and making no attempt to stop them abruptly. This is, of course, grossly patronizing. Nothing could be more calculated to make the tantrums ever worse and more destructive.

In principle, there are grounds for hoping that democratic states might develop in Africa. The tradition over much of the continent is of consensus politics rather than despotism. As happened earlier in Europe, developments have been from the tribal or ethnic level. Yet, though historically most modern democracies have been founded on nation-states, in Africa the accidental frontiers of the colonial period have resulted in many states which consist of a number of national groups welded together. In the long run, a new wave of nationalism may produce an epoch of further struggle in Africa, and we must be prepared to face such a situation.

Meanwhile, we should not make gratuitous attacks on states or regimes which we may influence by any other means; we should defend ourselves firmly but not aggressively if we are

unfairly criticized, and we should not countenance the idea
that, by describing itself as 'socialist', a Third World state is
entitled to superior moral claims. The Labour Party has to
some extent failed in this respect through linguistic confusion
as the 'socialism' often bears no resemblance to British socialism; (just as the 'liberal' constitutions of nineteenth century
Latin America were often little more than a gesture to the
political fashions of the time.)

Another error typical of left-wing well-wishers in the West is
to imagine that 'corruption' is particularly inherent in the more
'open', capitalist states of the Third World like Kenya, and that
states with high moral pretentions, progressive ideologies and
charismatic leaders are comparatively immune. This delusion
is based on the relative accessibility of information about such
countries, and the minor scandals of Kenya are no more,
perhaps, than natural imperfections in an otherwise fairly
sound economy. This contrasts with N'krumah's rule in Ghana
where many scandals became known only after his removal.
It emerged that the millions left in the treasury by the departing
British had disappeared; much of it had been spent on useless
prestige investments like jet liners, and a surprisingly large
amount on luxury cars for the liberator's mistresses.

Many American liberals also believed that, whatever its
faults, the Communist regime in Hanoi was not corrupt—unlike
those governments supported by the American troops. (Left-
wingers in 1939 and 1940 used to object to support for the
'corrupt' French Republic against Nazi Germany . . . .) On
the contrary totalitarian regimes are particularly susceptible to
corruption since they have no principle of regulating their
economic forces openly, but prefer suppression in favour of an
inefficient, administrative system. It is probably known by this
time, even among the Western left, that bribery is endemic in
the Soviet Union. Milovan Djilas tells us how in 1944 and 1945,
when the pure and devoted Yugoslav partisan leaders came
down from the mountains, there was an instant grab for all the
the economic perquisites. I was interested to read an article
about Vietnam in the *Washington Post** which quoted, at some

* Reprinted San Francisco *Sunday Examiner* and *Chronicle*, January 15,
1978

length, official Hanoi broadcasts and a special directive by the Communist Party's Central Committee Secretariat, on the subject of corruption; 'embezzlement, bribery, unlawful practices . . .' were mentioned not only in the newly-conquered South but in Hanoi, Haiphong and the Red River area in the North as well, often under the protection of 'ranking, influential officials'. The Party newspaper, *Nhan Dan*, alleged that on the rivers 'tons of fuel, cement, fertilizer, coal and grain' were being offered for sale. It appears that high officials are also making money by allowing refugees to leave at eight thousand dollars per family, and that corrupt bureaucrats succeed in having their accusers jailed instead of themselves.

All Third World countries are not necessarily as corrupt as Vietnam; and corruption without totalitatian terror is not as bad as corruption with it. A certain amount of corruption is no doubt inevitable: the West is not exempt. In any case, we have to deal with these governments if they are partially corrupt or partially despotic, and a number of them are not intrinsically hostile to the West; many are at least equally suspicious of the USSR. There is no reason for us to be discourteous or provocative in our relations. We should not conduct ourselves with the hostile clumsiness which the Left has shown even in diplomatic connexions, when dealing with countries like Chile. This is true of our relations even with the Communist states, and it is truer still when applied to Third World dictatorships with hostile tendencies towards us. On the other hand, we should defend our views, make it clear that we regard our system as greatly superior to its competitors, and—above all—answer all attacks firmly and forthrightly as soon as they are made.

All except the most fanatical Third World rulers will follow their own interests regardless. And the most fanatical—whose intransigence we should not underestimate—will be against us anyway.

Several misconceptions bedevil the consideration of how to ensure the rapid economic advance of Third World countries by aid and other methods of direct and indirect subsidy from the developed countries.

The 'Third World' covers a wide range of economies, from Kuwait (with the highest per capital income in the world) and the other oil nations, through powerfully developing economies like those of Malaysia or Brazil, to countries which are really poor. If we confine ourselves for purposes of Western aid to the last of these categories, (while providing encouraging trade terms for the second group) we find important divergences of opinion as to the best way of helping the advance towards prosperity.

At present, the idea of the 'North-South' relationship, in which the undeveloped countries demand and need special arrangements with the West to overcome their problems, has led them to accuse the West of having caused their poverty by colonialism, and perpetuated it by unfair trade arrangements. This is a fallacy: it is untrue that exploitation of Third World resources was the basis of Western economic ascendancy. On the contrary (as Professor Peter Bauer has said), 'the West was far ahead of the present Third World when it established contact with these regions in recent centuries'. The underdeveloped state of these countries today is not due to Western action, and even Marx recognized that the progress of the Third World was the direct result of the Western irruption. Bauer very cogently adds, 'Indeed, the very idea of material progress is Western'.

The contention that Western colonialism made the West rich at the expense of the Third World fails at both ends of the argument. Sweden and Switzerland, two of the world's richest countries, had no colonies at all, and little economic contact with the Third World area either. Portugal, which had a large empire in proportion to her size, is one of the poorest countries in Western Europe. Then again, the extremes of poverty are found precisely among those primitive peoples who had virtually no contact with the rest of mankind; and countries such as Afghanistan and Ethiopia, which were barely colonized, remain among the most backward.

The same principle applies to present day trade relations. Those countries listed in United Nations documents as least developed—Burundi, Chad, Lesotho, Ethiopia, Rwanda, Afghanistan, Bhutan, Nepal and Sikkim—are precisely those with the weakest trade relations with the West. On the other hand, countries like Malaysia, Venezuela, Taiwan, South

Korea, and the Ivory Coast, very closely connected to Western trading systems, are among the most developed.

In discussions about aid, the argument that a country is poor and backward and that this can be corrected by the transfer to it of large sums of money from countries which are richer and more developed, has only the merit of simplicity. It is easy to understand, and convincing as long as no searching questions are asked, for example: who gets the money? what is it spent on? and, above all, is there any evidence that the provision of money in this way has actually brought prosperity? But why are these questions not put, when their answers are known to contradict the original assumption? It seems to be partly rooted in the left-wing assumption that a State automatically invests its economic resources as productively as possible, a simple faith which many individuals in the Third World no longer share. (Part of Taiwan's economic success is undoubtedly due to the transfer, in 1954, of a number of large state enterprises to private ownership—cement, paper, machinery, mining and agricultural products were involved.)

There are certain areas in which the present apparatus of international committees and bureaucracies can be useful. It nevertheless seems true that the power of the state, or of several states together, to control and improve the productive forces is greatly exaggerated. The momentum of such attitudes tends to produce policies which in the long run are self defeating. What are we to make of, for example, the much publicized 'New International Economic Order', which advocates limiting the use of any new inventions in Western industry which diminish that industry's use of Third World products: that is to say, the internationalization of restrictive practices?

Countries which depend on the export of one or a few products are vulnerable to the movements of the world market, and there is a very good case for a system of cushioning the prices from international funds during recessions. But to go beyond this to a vast and permanent system of international planning is a step which needs to be approached with great care; and it alone cannot solve the more profound problems involved in radically improving the less developed economies of the World. Discrepancies between the rich and poor countries cannot be easily solved in the presence of the immense political and military pressure of the Soviet Union in the areas concerned, and with the concurrent encouragement—not only by the Communist countries—of bureaucratic étatisme, millennarian fanaticism and extreme nationalism.

Again, the pervasive notion that the Soviet model is suitable for turning backward countries into advanced industrial nations is totally wrong. Tsarist Russia was not backward in the sense in which we are speaking. And there is no evidence that communist planning methods have turned out well in any country. They managed to ruin the reasonably advanced Western economy of Czechoslovakia; and (in an adapted form) turned a Latin American country, Cuba, into an economic nightmare.

Senator Fulbright remarked in the Senate in April 1970,

> What on earth difference does it make to nomadic tribes of subsistence farmers in Vietnam or Laos or the North of Thailand whether they have a military dictator, a royal prince or a socialist commissar in some distant capital they have never seen and may never even have heard of?

This ludicrous assessment seems to be based on the idea that a communist regime makes no economic difference to the peasantry. This is, of course, totally untrue. Fulbright's 'subsistence farmer' is affected first by becoming a less-than-subsistence farmer, and then he becomes a *non*-farmer, a collectivized serf.

The only places where the problem of poverty has been solved to any significant degree are in the democratic industrial societies under capitalism. It is not true nowadays that poor countries are poor because rich countries are rich. American per capita production exceeds that of India by a greater proportion than American consumption per capita exceeds Indian consumption per capita. Yet, for a variety of confused reasons, we are constantly assured that poverty must be cured in the Third World, but that the only known method of doing this must be avoided. We are also told that the Western economies must, from their prosperity, pay large sums in aid to the backward countries, but at the same time they must abolish at home the same economies which make such aid possible. Those who speak like this want to have the fruits and to cut down the tree which bears them.

The practical tendency in ex-colonies is usually that which Yeats predicted when he wrote:

Parnell came down the road, he said to a cheering man:
'Ireland shall get her freedom and you still break stone.'

But where inappropriate ideology has gained a foothold, the last line should end like this:

. . . and you wish you still had the chance to break stone.

The Western 'capitalist' countries owe their prosperity to the political system, and the entire culture behind it. They should say so *but do not*—again leaving the field to those who support a one-party pseudo-socialism favourable to the Soviet Union. The backward countries will not achieve anything unless and until they have absorbed some of the Western principles, but this is no simple process.

If all the world's farmers operated like those of Britain or the United States, there would be no question of food shortages, even for a much larger population than the world has at present. Satellite photographs illustrate the effect of politics and culture with astonishing clarity. It might have been expected that Israeli frontiers should be clearly visible, or the US-Mexican border. But it is even the case that a clear-cut line divides the wholly comparable territories of Montana and Saskatchewan (the latter having a government moderately discouraging to private enterprise): it is even possible to trace the Texas-New Mexico line, Texas having a rather better system of agricultural bank loans. More directly to our point, a large green area is visible in the Sahel: it proves to belong to a French consortium which has not over-grazed the land.

The problem of farming livestock economically, to secure the optimum rather than the maximum number of cattle, is absolutely crucial to African development (just as destruction of the goat, effected in Israel but nowhere else in the Middle East, is vital for that area). In both cases the main problem is to change cultural attitudes, and this is not easily achieved. The interest of the USSR, in conjunction with indoctrinated local bureaucrats, is to abort such progress and introduce a neo-serfdom. We should make the issue clear in a forthright fashion, in our own interests and those of the Third World.

The way to bring the underdeveloped countries to the levels of prosperity achieved in the West is not by gifts, which at best put them in a parasitical relationship with the advanced country, but by policies which encourage the min the creation of advanced economies. Those Third World countries which see this, even in the absence of positive encouragement from the West (in particular Singapore, Hong Kong and Taiwan) have prospered. When Western money comes freely in the form of investment, that is the only sign that the economies are, or will be, viable. They get little public or political acclaim even in the West. It is agrogorod-crazy Tanzania which wins the applause.

The notion that the West is fulfilling its economic duty by merely passing money over is absurd. Foreign aid, in this primitive sense, is of little genuine help to the backward countries and its main effect is to give Western liberals a warm glow of satisfaction at their own generosity. (Occasions of immediate humanitarian need—famine in the Sahel or flood in the Sundarbans—are another matter: here the urgent purchase and supply of food and equipment are both right and sensible.) But generally, in this area of policy, the West has once more accepted rules incompatible with good sense, with its own interests, and with economic progress—and hence, in the long run, with world peace.

The question of aid is caught up in a very simple confusion. Willingness to pour money into a scheme to help a poor country—or a poor city or a poor category of citizens at home—is made the absolute criterion of humanity and decency, on the assumption that such action must automatically be helpful. This does not logically follow, and in most spheres there have been examples in which the intended results were not produced. Indeed, the 'liberal' who can so easily satisfy his conscience by giving away his fellow citizens' money should perhaps be told that it is a defect not of his intelligence but of his humanity that he does not care to consider the real results with more attention.

It is in part a product of this attitude, at once fawning and patronizing, that we find in fashionable attitudes to foreign aid. Professor Bauer and other prominent economists like the late Professor Harry Johnson of Chicago have pointed out that the whole concept of the advanced countries simply handing cash

over to the under developed countries contains a profound
fallacy. In the first place, of course, in a number of countries
(described by Bauer as 'Kleptocracies') the greater part of such
funds disappears into the pockets of the bureaucrats. In others
it is diverted into ideologically conceived and economically
worthless schemes. It may even be the case that major projects
which apparently look promising even to Westerners may contain the seeds of disasters. For example, the Aswan High Dam,
of which so much was expected, has already resulted in the
accumulation of the vital Nile silt where it is not wanted, the
lowering of the water table, and the spread of bilharzia . . .

In some of the West African countries state marketing boards
control the sale of the major part of agriculture. Their original
purpose was to stabilize the prices paid to the farmer. He sells
to the boards at prices set by them; and they then sell at the
world market. The intention was that when world prices were
high they would hold back part of the proceeds to provide a
reserve to pay out as part of the farmer's guaranteed price when
world prices were low. Assurances were given that no money
would be withheld from the producers. By 1962 these boards
had withheld between one third and one half of what they had
received on the world market, a total exceeding two billion
dollars. Since then reliable statistical information has not been
available.

On the other hand, if we look for developments worth encouraging, one of the really successful moves in the Third World
has been the growth of 'free trade zones' or 'export processing
zones'; in these areas imported raw materials and machinery
and exported finished products are excepted from customs
duties, bureaucratic procedures are greatly simplified and there
are other tax benefits. The economic successes of Taiwan, South
Korea and Malaysia in this field have led to imitation by all
except dogmatic 'Socialist' countries—though even there we
may note that mainland China's arrangements with the old
free port of Hong Kong constitutes one great exception. These
zones have since been established in the Philippines, and a
number of other countries—Gambia, the Ivory Coast, Kenya,
Senegal, Sri Lanka, Jamaica, and others are in various stages
of planning or discussion.

A thinking policy towards the Third World will consider the

cant of 'North-South' confrontation, and of aid, in the following terms. The West is richer than the rest of the world because of its political system, which made economic advance possible. Aid, in the form of handouts, is pouring money into the pockets of local bureaucrats. To reach Western consumption standards, countries must adopt Western production methods. Charity in floods and famines is one thing, but when giving real help to a developing country the main task is to encourage cultural changes. Prosperity has come to those countries which, like Singapore and Taiwan, have made investment attractive, rather than to those which have ruined their economies by ideas picked up at the London School of Economics or the Sorbonne, let alone the Patrice Lumumba University in Moscow. The whole vast structure of international aid is permeated with the fallacy of 'Etatisme'—the notion that governmental action is sufficient to produce wealth. I would not argue that there are no useful and important regulatory actions that governments may undertake, or that all the various elements in these new 'North-South' arrangements should be abandoned. I would, however, suggest that they be held under strict scrutiny, and that we should abandon the principle of state or inter-state manipulation as an automatic answer to problems.

This is not to recommend the total abolition of the international marketing bodies, nor the total cessation of 'aid', but rather to urge a careful scrutiny of those operations which are of doubtful utility, and the ending of those which—however well-intended—actively subsidize failure and regression. It is in everyone's interests to help the underdeveloped nations towards prosperity. But present attitudes and methods need radical change, and much more can be obtained for a far smaller and more productive investment. The British electorate, which understandably dislikes handing over large sums for useless purposes, in return for assorted curses, would also welcome this.

It is not the purpose of this book to deal with specific local problems of foreign policy, but those of the Middle East and of southern Africa constitute a danger possibly capable of triggering present major world-wide tensions. Policy in these danger areas faces many particular problems, but there are some general points worth making. It is usually the case that there is no satisfactory, clearcut solution which 'reserves the rights of all concerned, and sustains the interests of those opposed to Soviet expansionism.

For our opponents, the matter is simple. They support one side to the bitter end, and oppose all compromise; whereas we usually try to effect such a compromise by some makeshift arrangement acceptable, if only barely, to 'moderates' on both sides. We must recognize that, though principles must be maintained, there is often no practical way of preserving them in a pure state. There is nothing new in this. The right of self-determination of the Sudeten Germans in 1938 was incompatible in practice with the maintenance of the right of self-determination of the Czechs.

The problem of Israel presents difficulties which are seldom clearly faced. We may list them: (1) to reconcile the right to self-determination of the Arabs in the occupied territories with the existence of defensible Israeli borders; (2) to resolve the future of the Golan Heights. Here the doctrine that boundaries may not be changed leads to the absurd situation that Israel is asked to hand over an ideal jumping-off place for the drive of a heavily-equipped Syrian army to the sea. One should add that if the Arabs had won either of the last two wars, prospects would almost certainly not have been limited to the 1949 boundaries by the 'no annexation' doctrine. Moreover, while the present borders are merely armistice lines, the same was true of the 1949 borders, and these are no more likely to be sacrosanct. The West is in part to blame, for accepting without qualification the thesis that no boundaries may be changed by war. After all, many accepted European boundaries have no other basis. Quite apart from the results of World War II in Eastern Europe and (for example) the Soviet presence in Königsberg-Kaliningrad and Viipuri-Viborg, we may note the Italian-Austrian frontier of 1919, with Italians occupying the strategic line of the Alps and a German population under their control. Even more striking, perhaps, is the French annexation in 1945 of the Tende Valley in the Alps, a tiny mountain area quite comparable with the Golan Heights, which in the circumstances was obviously far less of a strategic danger.

Full Arab control of all the Arab lands of Palestine would put Israel in as powerless a strategic condition as was Czechoslovakia after German control of the Sudetenland. This is not to say that the Arabs are Nazis, but that some elements who might be in control would take any good opportunity to obliterate Israel. The problem is such that it does not seem to admit of a solution in the ordinary sense. Many solutions which are put forward are found to have omitted at least one important element from their calculations. Alternatively, a set of propositions may be formulated to cover every aspect of the problem; on discovering that no tidy solution emerges, we may yet be able to suggest the next best thing, a series of makeshifts, which may keep the peace on a year to year basis, by seeking whatever practical adjustments are possible between fundamentally irreconcilable positions.

Meanwhile, (as I write) Israel has put itself into the wrong with much of Western public opinion, by founding settlements not only on the West Bank, but in Sinai itself: and there has been no sign of a sensible approach to the problem of Jerusalem. Some form of Muslim, international or interreligious control of the Muslim holy places would do much to satisfy the Saudis for example. On the central issue, the only inducement for Israel to retire behind indefensible frontiers would be an iron-clad American or Western guarantee; but in present circumstances no guarantees are 'iron-clad'. One possible suggestion is that a American Military base would go far to secure a reliable US commitment.

As with Israel it may be appropriate not so much to suggest a 'solution' to the problems of southern Africa, as to note the difficulties in principle and in practice. In Africa it should be the policy of any sane Western government to prevent the expansion of the enemies of our culture to see that economically valuable and strategically significant areas do not fall under effecttive Soviet control. Such is our policy in Europe: and the whole of Asia and Africa cannot be handed over to the enemy without violently affecting the balance of power! The problems are, of course, interlocking and, in Africa, could have been tackled at the right tempo, and solutions found which are satisfactory to all concerned but for the intervention of the Communist states, as part of their strategy to overthrow the whole Western political culture. The intervention of an ideology which always claims to do everything better and quicker, tends anyhow to distort rational argument. When destructive ideas are supported

by the supply of arms and troops, the situation naturally becomes worse.

Yet we have advantages too. Many moderate Africans see the
rapid spread of the regimes of 'Leninists' gunmen, and who
note that these lead to terror, economic ruin, and above all the
slaughter of moderates like themselves. Indeed, this may apply
to some of those now regarded as extremists. It is not impossible
for nationalist revolutionaries of the most dedicated type to
accept a compromise giving them most but not all of their
demands. In Ireland, in the early 1920s, the majority of the
underground guerillas, headed by their leader Michael Collins
accepted less than total independence, less than the all of
territory they claimed, and conceded the continued presence of
British naval bases. And when the minority faction opposing
the Treaty faced them in civil war, they repressed it with great
ruthlessness. Some extremism has limited objectives.

The difficulty of applying formal democratic principles when
the differences between majority and minority are racial or
religious involves issues going beyond electoral counting.
Where the majority lacks rights, our sympathies must be with
that majority. On the other hand, minorities have rights too.
Whether in Ulster or in Rhodesia, admission of the minority's
rights should depend on the minority's admission of the
majority's rights. Solutions of varying equity include constitutional guarantees of 'power-sharing', or merely of the maintenance of the minority's full civil rights. Needless to say, the
choice between these is often made in an unbalanced manner.
The same people who want 'majority rule' in Rhodesia are
are opposed to it in Northern Ireland, where the minority
demand the 'power-sharing'. It will be very difficult to enforce
this against the feelings of the majority, particularly when the
allegiance of much of the minority is in effect to a foreign
country. Perhaps some convention could emerge by which
Catholics are given posts specially relevant to themselves—
possibly created for that purpose. They can already elect
officials and MPs in the areas in which they are the majority,
and their civil rights can be guaranteed against serious en-
croachment because they can be enforced from outside the area.

The problems of defending white minority rights in an
African country in which the black majority holds the instru-

ments of power are different in several respects. The most important is that no real sanction exists to enforce equity; when the white minority is economically more successful for historical reasons, a black leader needs rare long-sightedness to restrain his followers from killing the golden goose for short-term gain. However, it can be done—as in Kenya, though here the circumstances were rather different.

We are at a phase in human history when nationalism is regarded (except by Westerners) as legitimizing almost any kind of inflammatory action. It is understandable that no one wants to be a second-class citizen, and that there should be special difficulties when two of the nations involved are of different race and instantly distinguishable by skin colour. In spite of the high economic standards and civil liberties in South Africa compared with other areas, there is something peculiarly offensive about racial discrimination when it is raised to an ideological principle.

In Rhodesia, the original Anglo-American plan of insisting on the rule of guerillas who were supported (if not yet controlled) by Moscow was not acceptable to the majority of black Rhodesians. We must hope that the State Department and the Foreign Office may yet abandon this position—and perhaps send those who formulated the original idea, or any who still support it, to represent their countries in Paraguay or Bhutan.

During negotiations between Dr. David Owen and Mr. Andrew Young on the one hand and the self-appointed 'front-line states' on the other, there was little sign that the various strong options open to the Western negotiators were considered. Nothing, presumably, could be done about Marxist Angola and Mozambique, probably nothing about Tanzania. But there was every opportunity to lean hard on the more moderate Zambia and Botswana, whose real interests are clearly in accord with the non-Soviet solution of the Rhodesian issue. Indeed Zambia is a prime example of the lesson that there is nothing like effective action for winning or keeping friends. Zambia greatly desired Western intervention to prevent the Cuban takeover in Angola. It was only when we failed to provide it that Zambian relations with the West cooled off markedly.

It has been said that no settlement can work if the Soviet-supported guerilas do not accept it. On the contrary, no settlement can work if the Soviet-supported guerillas do accept it; for their acceptance would meant that they regarded it as ensuring that they would come to power, and would break it if they did not. This is precisely what happened in Angola, where all three parties accepted a coalition solution, until the Soviet-sponsored group found it possible to seize power on its own, with the support of Soviet-Cuban arms and troops.

In South Africa the difficulty with the 'panacea' of universal suffrage is the likelihood of the eventual rise to power of purely black parties; to ask them not to use their power against the economically more skilled and experienced whites would be to ask a lot. The opposite solution of 'homelands', in its present form, also seems unlikely to solve anything. Solutions which have worked elsewhere have included the exchange of populations, as between Greece and Turkey in the 1920s, and it is just possible to envisage a white withdrawal to the original area of settlement. The situation in Northern Ireland, with all its imperfections, is maintained as we have said by guarantee from outside the area. In Cyprus, the original 'cantonal' separation of the nations with an outside guarantee worked for a time, to the degree that the Turks would accept it for lack of a better alternative.

The very concept of a 'majority' claiming 'majority rule' is an admission of the existence in a given area of two nations, one larger than the other. The members of the larger nation claim to determine the fate of the smaller simply because there are more of them. If the nations are inextricably intermingled, the majority will normally gain power; but there is an excellent case in these circumstances for the minority having a separate electoral roll, separate representation, and constitutional guarantees against majority tyranny. The problem is the practical one of how to guarantee any of this: a 'consociational' arrangement with separate political nations co-ordinated only at the executive level, with mutual vetoes based on power and restraint, may seem most promising. At present prospects may not appear encouraging. At any rate, we should work for the rights of blacks, whites and others, in accordance with our principles and our interests, including the blocking of Soviet control.

In Ethiopia, the central problem for the West was and is

simply to prevent the Soviet Union establishing a firm base in the area. Such problems as reassuring Kenya against Somali irredentism complicate the matter but are in principle subsidary. There is no reason why an insistence on Soviet-Cuban withdrawal, backed by a firm threat to end all trade and other detente benefits to the USSR, could not have been coupled with a guarantee to Kenya. Given the will, the chance may recur.

And then, further north: the oil problem. This is so intricate and intractable because it is bound up with the Israeli situation in the Middle East, and complicated by Soviet pressure and penetration in the same area. Oil is not unique in that there are other raw materials—such as uranium—which are needed by the advanced countries but obtainable mainly from non-Western areas. It is not necessarily a permanent problem: Britian's own oil resources may transform our situation, and there are possibilities in the American shale beds; the resources of the older oil producers are likely to peter out in decades; and the prospects of other energy sources are reasonably good. However, for the immediate future the advanced countries (especially Japan) are in principle at the mercy of boycotts and are forced to pay an uneconomic price for fuel. The vast flow of wealth to some of the oil countries like Libya may also result in a build-up of trouble for the future.

There is an element in OPEC which realizes that prices cannot be forced up indefinitely, and at the same time that profits, beyond a certain point, are of use only as an investment in the West; prominent OPEC regimes are suspicious of, and hostile to Soviet expansionism, but some of these regimes are not very stable. The debacle in Iran may, at inordinate cost, produce a serious understanding of the dangers. The Persian Gulf is one of the few areas for which the American Secretary for Defence has publicly required his forces to maintain an operational readiness. This is at least a recognition that national necessity must override other considerations if the worst comes to the worst.

Yet an alliance which does not match or over-match the Soviet Union militarily will need both coolness and firmness to intervene in an area so close to its adversery's main strengths. The dangers would be much reduced if the West turned to a sounder armament policy and prepared to take a firmer political line in such areas as the Indian Ocean and the Horn of Africa. This applies throughout the Third World, a few of whose characteristic problems we have briefly considered.

10

The Home Front

As Zbigniew Brzezinski has remarked (*Newsweek*, 26 April 1971), in foreign affairs

> will becomes the crucial variable: one must have enough power to change the potential enemy's intentions while preventing one's own determination from crumbling.

Brzezinski went on to say that 'National will' is an essential which some think cannot subsist here, at least in sufficient strength to counterbalance the more easily mobilized willpower of a totalitarian machine. There is no reason to believe this. The reader may recall Richard Hillary writing in 1940 of his motives as a fighter pilot that he wanted to prove that sceptics like himself could make headway against the 'dogma-fed youth' of the Luftwaffe. And he and his colleagues produced the proof. That spirit survives in spite of years of denigration. But it needs to be harnessed and encouraged.

A successful foreign policy must rely, in a democratic country, on popular understanding and support. In Britain, the general instincts of the population are sound. There is a traditional dislike and suspicion of the totalitarian systems, an unsympathetic attitude towards the Soviet Union, a growing understanding of the threat posed by the Soviet armed forces, and a willingness to support a higher level of armament by the United Kingdom.

This last may remind us that if the country's government must depend on the springs of public will to give realization to sound policy, this will is not entirely spontaneous. The country's instincts need clarification and leadership from the politically responsible. During the past few years serious public discussion of the armament question has led to a well-justified state of alarm at the way things are going. (This is also true in the United States.)

The notion that the public can only be moved by economic issues is false. When the British were considerably poorer than they are today, this did not prevent them from taking a keen and serious interest in the essentials of foreign policy, and in particular of defence. Everyone understood that the Kaiser's navy had a single real mission, the destruction of Britain: just as everyone understands that the Soviet armament is levelled menacingly at Britain and her allies today. Seventy years ago, a Conservative could win a by-election in a working class district on the issue of building enough Dreadnoughts—'We want eight, We won't wait'—and indeed forced the Liberal government to expand its naval programme.

There seems no doubt that Mrs. Thatcher's foreign policy speeches have captured the instinctive common sense of the majority of the nation. The arguments mobilized against her position, generally speaking, assert that it is unsophisticated and simplistic. In reality, it is the left-wing or appeasement view which is based on weak arguments, while the Thatcher approach is in accord with a most profound understanding of the particular problems of foreign policy which face us. Yet it would be fair to say that the patriotism and common sense implicit in this attitude have lacked a well developed philosophical basis and so remain vulnerable to sophistical attack. This is a want which would not be tolerated in economic and social affairs. The weakness of the patriotic position traditionally common to all three parties is that few of those in political life who subscribe to it have done much thinking or writing on foreign policy. The Left, on the other hand, swarms with producers of analysis and opinion on these matters, who are wrong-headed and essentially shallow, but disproportionately influential and full of the power to distract others from reality.

Patriots themselves are not immune from comfortable delusions, when they lack adequate guidance. Among them there are people who think they understand foreign affairs, without having made the real intellectual and imaginative effort required. And in the Foreign Office there is this tendency to regard negotiation and the search for concession, as desirable in themselves and more central to fruitful relations than a grasp of the essentials. This situation is highly dangerous for the West as a whole, and is far more critical than any other political problem.

There is a striking similarity of view among serious students of the USSR that the Soviet leaders remain in a state of total enmity towards the West, which they only fail to translate into action when they are prevented from doing so. But there are not many serious students of the USSR of any repute; and most of them are academics without a powerful involvement in foreign policy matters, however telling their occasional interventions on the press. It is natural enough that most members of Parliament are not foreign policy experts, and that solid thinking is not found everywhere in the press and on television. There are public men with a clear idea of the Soviet threat, among them those carrying out or making use of studies of defence policies. But a gap remains between the political world and the more profound analysis of Soviet and other motives on which foreign policy must lay its philosophical foundations.

The comfortable view, common in political circles, holds that the Soviet leaders are 'reasonable men' and only need to be treated nicely; this is based on the fallacy that they have the same motivations as ourselves. We must not project our own assumptions on to a totally different political culture, to which they do not apply. Clear thinking on this point can teach and train the will.

The will of the nation is not a simple concept. The vague patriotism of the people has to be translated into clear and articulate positions on the vital issues by political leaders. Thus we depend greatly on their willpower and clear-mindedness. The political class overlaps with and is sensitive to the views of a wide range of journalists, and other 'intellectuals'. The prevailing mood among the latter is often inappropriate to modern reality and reflects intellectual fashions and factions which have long since become obsolete. This is the case with many domestic issues, such as education and welfare; and it is even more persistent on matters which impinge less directly on the individual in question.

Critical thought on politics, beginning with the predecessors of Socrates, provides a major contrast between our society and the despotisms. It is useful to distinguish between the 'precritical' societies and the critical ones which, in some cases, followed. Only the Western type of society, just as it managed to create a strong state without destroying a consensus, managed to contain the critical attitude without destroying the older, less 'rational' loyalties. In this it was invariably hampered by those who were determined to conceptualize, rationalize, and verbalize everything, (mainly academics and members of early-teenage debating societies, from the time of the Sophists and their pupils on. Athenian critical examination of society produced some advantageous results, but also led to a farrago of foolish talk and frigid paradox, which was enormously attractive to some types of mind, and is fully comparable to what we have today. The Sophists envisaged the post-critical society as one in which every view or decision is the product of pure reason; they treated the old half-conscious bonds and myths which united that society as insignificant. But the bonds of social order did not become entirely conscious; they could not, any more than the development in the human animal of the consciousness or self-awareness which distinguishes him from other species eliminated the person unconscious.

Political civilization subsists both at a rational level and at a depth beyond present—perhaps any—analysis, as with successful art appealing, in A. E. Housman's words,

> to something in man which is obscure and latent, something older than the present organization of his nature, like the patches of fen which still linger here and there in the drained lands of Cambridgeshire.

Political civilization consists of attachment to the tradition of generations. It is an attitude both modern and libertarian, open to the seeking of undogmatic solutions to unforseen problems. This modern style has not deprived itself of the barbarous strength of the ancient loyalties; it cannot survive if it does so. As Orwell said, during World War II (in his *Wells, Hitler and the World State*):

> What has kept England on its feet during the past year? In part, no doubt, some vague idea about a better future, but chiefly the atavistic emotion of patriotism, the ingrained feeling of the

English-speaking peoples that they are superior to foreigners. For the last twenty years the main object of English left-wing intellectuals has been to break this feeling down, and if they had succeeded, we might be watching the S.S. patrolling the London streets at this moment.

The emergence of the mind did not lead to the disappearance of the heart. And this is the essential of any genuine progress. As Whitehead put it: 'Those societies which cannot combine reverence to their symbols with freedom of revision, must ultimately decay'. The patriotism of the West is not solely a tribal solidarity, but a feeling for the 'nation', and also for the order. Men who do not deny their past are wiser than men who do or who try to. As Burke wrote (in his *Reflections on the Revolution in France*), in the English Petition of Right

> The parliament says to the king, 'Your subjects have *inherited* this freedom', claiming their franchises not on abstract principles 'as the rights of men', but as the rights of Englishmen, and as a patrimony derived from their forefathers.

Nor were Selden and the other learned men who drew up the Petition ignorant of the many general theories then already current about 'the rights of man'. They simply preferred to ground themselves upon experience, rather than enter the vague and wild territory of speculation. The same could be said about the American Founding Fathers. Arthur Schlesinger, Sr. remarked that they were 'men of vision without being visionaries'; Carl Bridenbaugh that they were 'men of intellect, not intellectuals'.

In the long run, our own political culture depends less on the conscious will of our statesmen and citizens, or on our political institutions, than on trends, traditions and habits, unconscious as much as conscious, unformulated as much as legislated. As Aristotle noted (in *The Politics*),

> There are plenty of instances of a constitution which according to its law is not democratic, but which owing to custom and way of upbringing is democratic in its workings; there are likewise others which according to law incline towards democracy, but by reason of custom and upbringing operate more like oligarchies.

And, of course, one does not transcend one's culture, one simply deserts it. As Orwell said, patriotism is for better or for worse. Stephen Decatur's famous words (now frequently given in a later and perverted form), 'Our country! In her intercourse with foreign nations, may she always be in the right; but our country right or wrong', do not state a general principle, but only assert that in a society of the Western democratic type involvement is inextricable. Those who go outside it are not judging from a superior position; they have merely cut their roots. And the conclusions they reach are not purely rational and moral: rather, they represent the rationalization either of active hostility to the soil that has nourished them, or, (less disreputable though more silly) of the childish hope for short cuts to perfection, the provision by magic of peace, or plenty, or justice. In any case intellectuals delude themselves when they think that they can be detached from these feelings, can stand above such things and judge from the point of view of abstract principles. As Orwell pointed out, they quickly became attached simply to another, and hostile, 'nationalism', by which he means allegiance to some different principle.

Decatur's formulation is quite unlike the nationalism we are accustomed to from the states in which it is associated with ideological fanaticism. With them, the mere possibility of being 'wrong' does not arise: their 'right' is *defined* in terms of their own allegiance. The distinction between patriotism and nationalism can perhaps best be made on the following basis: patriotism is self-assured, deep, fully rooted in the unconscious and its assumptions, and is derived from the general traditions in the society working in each psyche. It is a judgement less of the outside world than of one's own culture. Nationalism is a more recent, less self-assured, more artificial product, and one of its main components is envy, suspicion and hostility to others; part of its basic motivation is its attitude to other cultures. It is necessary to whip it up continually; in war its armies need constant hate propaganda to sustain them.

Gibbon, in a famous passage, asserted that the West was in little danger of the fate that overtook Rome. It was no longer probable, he said, that the steppe could produce hordes of barbarians adequate to overthrow the prosperous realms of

Europe, whose resistance would be firm. But in case of disaster in Europe he saw one final safety measure in mass emigration to the Americas, which, it then appeared, no enemy could reach. Nowadays, we may feel that he underestimated the steppe, not forseeing Herzen's 'Genghiz Khan with the Telegraph'— and with the Intercontinental Ballistic Missile. But he also underestimated, indeed hardly thought of, the internal Goth.

The attitudes which lead to a perverse view of communist despotism and aggression are various, not all of them wholly disreputable in origin. Albert Camus noted of French Stalinists sympathizers that they did not so much like the Russians as 'heartily detest part of the French'. Hitler always congratuated himself that his problem was one of coming to power in a land 'already soaked in Marxism': that is, a Germany in which reason and balance had been eroded. Despotism from the East has encouraged factions in the Western states since the time when Spartans and Athenians 'medized'. (It is a curious parallel, too, that the Great King and his rivals found it suitable to import Western military and other techniques.) Thus, there are Britons who are able to forget that the Soviet regime has suppressed socialists, unorthodox communists, strikers and small nations, and only remember that 'capitalists' were also among the victims. These left-wing ideologues declare that they are loyal to Britian—to a different, better, newer Britain, a sort of fog-bound Cuba. But in reality, as Orwell noted, Britain is very resistant to alien life forms, and such a takeover is advocated only in very narrow, though noisy, circles. We may be reminded of the Church of England's old Prayer Book form of Thanksgiving for the Restoration, in which it condemns 'traterous, heady and high-minded men'.

Yet it is not the extreme examples which count, so much as the well-meaning man or woman in theory alienated from his society, at least to the extent of claiming to be an impartial judge between it and its opponents; the 'liberal' who is playing God, or Marx. He deploys a critical attitude of the type, which, as Canning wrote,

> spares its foes; nor e'er descends
> With bigot zeal to combat for its friends.

He often deplores the actions of the USSR, and is not a partisan of despotism, but nevertheless his first principle is criticism of his own country. There is plenty to criticize in Britain or the USA, or in any society. In a sense, the failings are more obvious than elsewhere—just as eczema is more obtrusive, more visible than cancer of a vital organ. But people who seriously compare the West and its faults, troubles and problems with those of the totalitarian countries as if they were equal (or even as if the West was worse), are simply talking nonsense. They are stuck in shallow verbalism, a world reducible to debating society terms, where a man can live without roots, making all his decisions about political, social, literary and other matters simply on the basis of how an argument on one side of such an issue may convince him at a given moment—to be reversed later, on hearing a better or more polysyllabic debater.

The Western mind is confused by the presentation of two different ethical attitudes on matters of foreign affairs. The first is exemplified by those scientists who refuse to take part in any research which might help to kill people. On the face of it, this is a position of simple and dazzling ethical purity and is represented as such, with much self-congratulation, in the circles where it is held. The idea of defending the democratic culture scarcely arises.

Those who hold other attitudes believe that abstract principles are not sufficient when dealing with the real world; that without extremely powerful defences and deterrents our hard-won liberties and values would be lost perhaps irretrievably, and that the human race might possibly be wiped out; that purity of motive is not enough, (the road to hell is paved with good intentions), and above all that it is crucial to study the results of our action, or failure to act.

It is a curious anomaly that it is the holders of the first view who speak of being 'concerned', the assumption being that sufficient goodwill and 'concern' on the part of the commentator guarantee the correctness of his views. Scientists should not need to be told that the intensity of their convictions is no measure of either their correctness or their possible good effects: Torquemada was far more certain of his rightness and righteousness than was David Hume.

Some intellectuals become so hostile to their own society that they are effectively blinded to the frightfulness of the alternatives. This is not the place to analyse their motives, but these are probably best explained in a letter Einstein once wrote to Freud about the difficulty of eliminating hate and destructiveness from the human psyche. He commented:

> Here I am thinking by no means only of the so-called uncultured masses. Experience proves that it is rather the so-called intelligentsia that is most apt to yield to these disastrous collective suggestions, since the intellectual has no direct contact with life in the raw but encounters it in its easiest synthetic form—the printed page.

The true 'liberal' is almost invariably misinformed about foreign affairs, even more than he is mininformed about his own country. It is easy to maintain a stereotype about another country and culture, as fewer and better-selected facts filter through. There are always like-minded people who will ensure that reality is censored, sorted out and labelled before dispatch to the homeland; that an easily digestible pap is substituted for the analysis of situations which are frequently tough and complex, and would require an intellectual effort to master without some such processing. The result can be a disastrous compound of ignorance and malice. (A prominent and pampered actress from Hollywood once remarked to a friend of mine that Stalin's trouble lay in not killing enough people.)

This has applied even to the last War. Hostility to the Western democratic culture now requires that British and American actions in World War II be equated with those of the Nazis, Dresden being as bad as Auschwitz. Not much is made of the point that when we had our enemies at our mercy we did not put them all in gas-chambers. Indeed the main emphasis of blame for Auschwitz itself is often put on criminal neglect by the Allies.

Old issues of a purely political nature are, of course, kept alive. The epithet 'Men of Munich' was long used against certain Conservatives. (Though the morally exact parallel by which anti-Munichites urged that the Baltic States be handed over to Stalin is rarely mentioned.) The errors are obvious to anyone who has studied history. They have resulted in attempts to replace genuine history with fantasy, in the various 'revisionist' books which try to show that Truman, or Baldwin, were the true villains of the century.

One of the trends of thought which may lead to useless or dangerous decisions is often based on genuine concern and compassion, but this is not always supported by the awareness of a responsibility to investigate and establish what are the *real* results of charitably intended actions. When plans go wrong there is a tendency to blame the established order in one's own country and to seek fine-sounding comprehensive solutions. In internal affairs organizations which are devoted to genuine good work may be misled in this way: for example, societies like Shelter, which tries to help the homeless, go beyond this and urge political and social policies which sound good but provide no real solutions. Similar examples may be seen in foreign affairs where Oxfam is devoted to relieving hunger in the world, but has become entangled in social and political ideas which promise a lot but do not relieve hunger. Apart from the tendency of these men of good will to accept political actions which often turn out to be highly destructive, they are also likely to be affected by a general good will which sees the best in every culture but our own. And so they feel that armaments piled up in defence against people who are really quite nice are pointless, or wicked.

The 'liberal' has a humane hatred of war and the sufferings it causes. Though he may know in principle that the sufferings of war are not always as bad as the sufferings of certain types of peace, he seldom follows this train of thought to its logical conclusion—particularly if he only hears of the horrors, true or false, on the pro-Western side of any conflict. For this and other reasons, we find an influential section of the community which tends to erode the will of the West. Of course they are not Communists, and some of them are even in a sense anti-communist. It is just that they want a bi-partisan foreign policy with the Communists.

One can, for example, often see them signing petititions or letters in which the political geologist can find, among their co-signatories, stratum after stratum of earlier lunacies: writers who, in the thirties, signed manifestos attacking those who cast doubt on the Moscow trials: scientists who, in the forties, called Stalin a Coryphaeus of Science; poets who, in the fifties, held that North Korea was attacked by South; actors who, in the early sixties, supported the Soviet missile bases in Cuba. The new recruits either do not know this or do not care, and show a level of imprudence they would scarcely sink to if their own interests were concerned. At least, they do not put their own savings in projects to buy Brooklyn Bridge or shares in pearl mines.

This whole attitude to world affairs can be summed up in the satirical exchange:

Q: Now that fighting is going on between Cambodia and Vietnam, which country should be called a threat to peace?
A: Chile.

In addition to the philanthropic but shallow-minded 'liberal', (and often united with him in an unnatural alliance), we find true supporters of the Soviet system—notably among the National Executive Committee of the Labour party.

The intricate manipulation by minorities of parts of the Labour party machinery has produced a situation in which the Labour voters, (the vast majority being loyal, patriotic and anti-totalitarian), are saddled with a National Executive Committee (NEC) which, far from having any objection to the Soviet system, consorts openly with its most Stalinist representatives like Boris Ponomarev. Here, among some of the trade union leaders and in some of the constituency parties are groups whose exposure ought to become one of the concerns of British foreign policy. It is not a question of Left or Right: there are many whose political views are far to the Left, who are nevertheless quite clear about the Soviet threat (for example, the Maoist parties on the Continent). Many also of the more traditional Left have always been clear on these issues.

Communism's relations with Social democracy have gone through many periods in which a wooing approach has temporarily replaced, or coexisted with, violent attacks. The basic principle of this co-operation was Lenin's public remark that the Communists would support the British Labour party 'as the rope supports the hanged man'. Most socialist leaders have understood this. As Aneurin Bevan wrote in 1951:

> The Communist party is the sworn inveterate enemy of the socialist and democratic parties. When it associates with them, it does so as a preliminary to destroying them. There is an old German aphorism which says: 'To cast an enemy out it is first necessary to embrace him'. That is what the Communists mean when they ask for cooperation and alliance with the Socialists . . . The Communist does not look upon a Socialist as an ally in a common cause. He looks upon him as a dupe, as a temporary convenience, and as something to be thrust ruthlessly to one side when he has served his purpose.

This was in an introduction to *The Curtain Falls*, a book edited by Dennis Healey, telling the story of the fate of the Polish, Hungarian and Czechoslovak social democrats. In the intervening period the communist leaders (with the sole exception of Imre Nagy in the last days of the Hungarian Revolution in 1956) have never given any sign of making restitution, or even expressing regret for the crushing of these social democratic parties. Of course, in the international field, the establishment of peaceable relations with the communist states is in the general interest of all governments. But to go on from there and think in terms of a special bond between communists and social democrats is to fall into error.

Of the five demands made by Brezhnev and the Soviet Politburo to Dubcek and the Czechoslovak Communists at the Cierna-nad-Tisu meeting, four were specific attacks on persons or groups then active in Prague. Only one was of a general nature: an insistence that the Czechoslovaks should promise not to legalize the Social Democratic Party.

An even more extraordinary example of this Communist attitude was given a few years ago in *Der Spiegel* (reprinted in *Encounter*, August 1971). In an interview, Dr. Eduard Goldstücker was asked if the Czechoslovak Social Democratic Party might not have been allowed to re-emerge in 1968. He said no, since they had had nothing to offer. When it was suggested that the electorate might decide that, he did not budge and said that Social Democrats did not want what he regarded as socialism. It was again suggested that even so, the Czechoslovak working class might be allowed the choice, but he again rejected the whole idea on the grounds both that the Social Democrats would remain a small sect and that they would represent a danger.

Dr. Goldstücker played an outstanding role in the Dubcek 'Prague Spring'. If the idea of tolerating social democrats is wholly alien, even to such a notable 'liberal' communist, this shows how deeply rooted is the antagonism of communism towards social democracy.

So why do the NEC and its supporters admire, and wish for comradely party relations with the Communist Party of the Soviet Union, when one of the latter's leading principles is to suppress democratic socialists? The answer can only be, surely, that they are not democratic socialists, and do not care what happens to those who are. Their allegiance is to a 'socialism' of which the Soviet Union is an example.

The fate of the Eastern European socialist and social democratic parties was partly due to the fact that they had pro-communists and secret Communists in their ranks, working closely and clandestinely with, or under the control of, the Communist party. Zdenek Fierlinger, who betrayed the Czechoslovak Social Democratic Party and was rewarded with a high post in the Communist Party, tells in his memoirs how even before the liberation of Czechoslovakia at the end of the war, and without the knowledge of the Social Democratic Party leadership, his group held discussions with the Communists to co-ordinate action. Similarly, Ronai, prominent in the group which betrayed the Hungarian Social Democratic Party, tells us in his memoirs that he had been a secret Communist all the time. It seems unlikely that such tactics have been eschewed in the case of our own socialist parties.

Meanwhile when a moderate Labour leadership is able to maintain the general principles of the Western alliance, it is always under immense pressure from the Left. Whenever no real concessions can be made to the Left on internal matters without the instant ruin of the economy, there is a special temptation to appease them by verbal abuse of, and active 'policy' measures against bugbears such as Pinochet and Ian Smith. It sometimes seems, indeed, that a 'moderate' Labour leader who has had to come to terms with reality in the areas covered by his own experience, may often nourish a similar animus to that of the Left in foreign policy, this being the one area in which his residual ideological illusions can be safely indulged. This has several disadvantages: first, attention is distracted from the really major issues. Policy is distorted so that we find ourselves backing Soviet-sponsored factions against our own interests and principles; and the encouragement of the factious left-wing uproar in this country tends to confuse public opinion.

There are those who take the view, 'better Red than dead', urging that surrender at least means 'peace'. Not so. There is every indication that a fully communist world would be one of frightful conflicts. In 1944 Milovan Djilas heard from a Soviet Army Commander a suggestion which was 'strange to me then': the Russian had come to the conclusion that 'when communism triumphed in the whole world, wars would then take on a final bitterness'. Though this idea was strange to Djilas at the time, he came to agree that

> various sects would undertake the reckless destruction of the human race for the sake of its greater 'happiness'.

Within four of five years, the first inter-communist war had reached an advanced planning stage. The British fellow traveller, Konni Zilliacus, tells us in his memoirs, on the authority of the Czech Stalinist Vice-Premier Fierlinger, that the Hungarian dictator Rakosi had made preparations to invade Yugoslavia. Needless to say, this was not an independent initiative, but a plan of Stalin's. It appears that the operational plan for the invasion had already been prepared on Stalin's orders, by General Shtemenko, (later Chief of Staff of the Warsaw Pact): it was only abandoned when leading Soviet Marshals examined it and took the view that it would lead to military disaster on the lines of the Finnish war of 1939–40. The reason Stalin could not afford a long campaign was political —the existence of the West, of the 'capitalist' world. And Tito's adherence to the Balkan Pact, the then military defence alliance with the anti-communist states of Greece and Turkey, shows that he understood this point.

In 1956 the first inter-communist war actually took place, in Hungary. A Government headed by the Hungarian Communist Party was overthrown after bitter fighting by the troops of the Soviet Communist Party. At the same time, a more dangerous situation developed in Poland, where Soviet troops moved on the Polish capital and were blocked by the Poles. Here, a compromise was only reached because the Polish army was much larger than that of Hungary, and the Poles were determined to fight even if it produced an European war. The invasion of Czechoslovakia in 1968 did not lead to fighting, because the Czechs did not resist; but the Russians were clearly prepared to crush them if they had.

On the Russian-Chinese border, series of minor armed clashes led in 1969 to a full scale battle on the Ussuri, (a curious parallel with the similar large but localized battles between Japanese and the Soviet forces in the same area in July-August 1938). It is now reasonably clear that for several years thereafter, the USSR was on the brink of a 'preventive' war against China, involving nuclear weapons—and that, once again, war would have been certain but for the existence of the non-communist world. For while non-communist states exist, they exercise a restraining influence. First, to attack China with the West intact would carry obvious risks. Second, the Western populations provide a world public opinion of which the Soviet leaders must take some cognisance since they eventually hope to make use of it in achieving further gains. In a communist world, where public opinion need no longer be taken into account, such a sanction would not apply.

I had written the above before the outbreak of severe fighting between communist Vietnam and communist Cambodia was reported. Perhaps the proof is now adequate. There are already many people in South East Asia who may have hoped that, whatever its faults, a communist regime would at least mean peace of a sort, but who are now both red and dead.

People nowadays form their opinions of a foreign state largely on the basis of the number of 'atrocities' reported of it. The key word here is clearly 'reported'. The loser, in terms of

Western opinion, is not the state that commits the most atrocities so much as the one whose enemies have the best propaganda machine. For such reports, however impressive, are quite without value if provided by the tightly organized adherents of a millenarian ideology, who are dedicated in principle to the idea that political advantage to their side is the highest moral criterion and takes automatic precedence over such values as truth. There is no way of establishing the truth of such allegations.

This thirst for atrocities is, as always, satisfied by a large corps of pushers. Arthur Koestler describes how Willy Muenzenberg (himself later to be killed by the NKVD) organized the Communist propaganda operation in the West in the thirties, together with his subordinate Otto Katz (also later executed, in Prague) and Koestler himself. Koestler, then a member of the Communist Party, had posed as a liberal in his capacity as Spanish war correspondent of the liberal *News Chronicle* (his two fellow correspondents in Spain, William Forrest and John Langdon-Davies were also crypto-communists). When he was captured by the Nationalists, Katz devised fictitious stories about his ill-treatment in prison, and a great campaign was aroused to secure his release, supported by Conservative M.P.'s and others. (The British Communist Claud Cockburn has revealed in his autobiography that, at this time, he too was devising an entirely false account of a rising against Franco in Tetuan.) But Muenzenberg, the Comintern's propaganda genius, was not content with mere factual falsifications. He criticized Katz and Koestler:

> He would pick up a few sheets of the typescript, scan through them, and shout at me: 'Too weak. Too objective. Hit them! Hit them hard! Tell the world how they run over their prisoners with tanks, how they pour petrol over them and burn them alive. Make the world gasp with horror. Hammer it into their heads. Make them *wake up*'.

Such an attitude has become traditional. We can be reasonably sure today that many of the allegations fed into our press by totalitarian party machines are equally dubious.

After the Vietnam War with its vast output of anti-American

atrocity propaganda (much of which is now proved to have been faked in Hanoi and fed direct to Western 'peace' activists), it was ironic to read, in January 1978, the following statements by rival Communist regimes, which were directed not against the wicked imperialists but against each other:

> They have perpetrated utterly inhuman crimes—raping, tearing fetuses from mothers' wombs, disemboweling adults and burning children alive. (Vietnamese Premier Pham Van Dong.)

> They have strafed children and old folks, burned houses, seized cattle . . . raped and killed our women. (Cambodian Chairman Khieu Samphan.)

The central idea in all these cases is to arouse such a high level of moral indignation that no argument on the merits of the case is required, like a jury which treats the abominable nature of a crime as a reason for not considering the evidence fairly, since so fearful an act must not go unpunished. If our blood boils enough, we do not have to think. For a generation abominable acts have been committed all over the world, and they should be thoroughly investigated. In some areas, which are in the grip of radical social or racial ideologies, such acts are not merely emergency measures directed against immediate and dangerous political enemies, but part of a vast scheme of oppression directed against whole sections of the population. It has taken thirty years for the truth about the Stalin terror to become generally accepted in the West. More recent regimes on the same principles have only been in power for ten or twenty years, and can presumably count on a further period of grace so long as their denials are suitably phrased. Just as (in Kipling's words) 'there are more things told than are true, there are more things true than are told'.

In general, the more easily a malpractice can be reported on, the less repressive the regime. This is true even within the Communist bloc. The fact that a fair amount of information is now available on the sufferings of the opposition in the USSR, while this is not so of North Korea, indicates that the present Soviet regime is the less repressive of the two. This is in accordance with the general rule that the very worst regimes of our time have been able to suppress much of the truth about their activities by the extreme rigour of their control. Round the world today, the countries which are most often featured in the media as the leading centres of atrocity are not necessarily those which are really the worst. Of course, Stalinism did not prevent a good deal of information coming out: but those determined to be duped in the West were able to reject or (in psychological terms) repress this bad news, because they were offered a clear-cut alternative story, and no way could be found of checking the information, except through emigres who were naturally labelled as anti-Soviet and therefore unreliable.

Unfortunately, it can hardly be said that a tendency to temper the wind to the unshorn wolf has disappeared from the 'progressive' community. For example, the regime in Chile is clearly oppressive. We may all hope for a fairly rapid return to democracy (though not to the alleged 'democracy' of those much touted emigres who really stand for another, and, on the record far more unpleasant, dictatorship).

The authoritarian regime of the Colonels in Greece was almost unprecented in having executed no one during the period immediately following the seizure of power. Every liberal would have agreed that Yugoslavia was and had long been far less oppressive; it was only by a turn in the power struggle that we learnt that at the beginning of the sixties Rankovich, Yugoslav Minister of the Interior, was having people shot by the score throughout the towns and villages of the Kosmet. Nor is Yugoslavia a particularly bad example.

In general, a much more critical attitude is required about the whole 'atrocity game'. George Orwell, a supporter of the Spanish Republican cause who fought and was wounded in its battles, nevertheless wrote that for him the most horrifying thing about that war was not the violence on the spot, but the immediate retreat of the Western Left into what he called 'the mental slum' of atrocity story-mongering, and he added:

> whether such deeds were reprehensible, or even whether they had happened, was always decided according to political predilection.

Having once chosen sides internationally, people are conditioned to believe any case against their enemies and disbelieve any case against their friends. A former editor of a British left-wing journal described how, hitherto uninterested in politics, he saw in a Paris riot a right-wing policeman kicking a left-wing girl in the stomach. Instead of concluding that policemen shouldn't kick girls in the stomach, he concluded that right-wingers shouldn't kick left-wingers in the stomach . . .

Stockholm is, of course a regular plague spot of this 'double-think': not only its Social-democrats, and its be-Myrdalled committees, but its World Council of Churches, the Marxist theologians of whose *apparat* are always silent about the pleas of the Catholics of Lithuania and the Baptists of Siberia, while accepting the state-fed Soviet clerics of whom Solzhenitsyn has so eloquently complained.

The liberal conscience, admirable in principle, is liable to strange aberrations in practice, especially—as we have noted—when it gets involved in organizations. That well-intentioned body, Amnesty International, is a case in point: it produced a hostile report on British atrocities in Aden, and no one protested when its investigator turned out to be a 'Swedish' doctor with an Arab name who had got no further than Cairo. With the swing of one section of left-wing opinion against Israel, there came a crop of alleged Israeli atrocities. There is nothing impossible about an Israeli committing an atrocity. But after months of investigation, in which Amnesty men traversed the length and breadth of Israeli-held territories, questioning prisoners, no evidence was unearthed. However, Amnesty then published four anonymous 'case histories', based on unchecked and uncorroborated statements made by Arab refugees outside Israel. The Israeli government offered to investigate. (Earlier allegations when checked had been found to be untrue.) We cannot say that no malpractices took place, but by totalitarian standards they can only have been on a very small scale.

One Amnesty expert who was covering the case of conscientious objectors throughout the world, was able to point to their sufferings in the countries of the West, including Switzerland; however in Russia, while it seemed that 'a small number' were similarly imprisoned for the offence, nothing definite could be stated because 'it has proved impossible to obtain more definite information' . . . Many people, including Amnesty, seem to be confused about 'prisoners of conscience'! One often finds that demands are made with equal strength for the liberation on the one hand of a Russian imprisoned for complaining about the conduct of the trial of another Russian accused of writing a piece of undesirable fiction, and on the other for the liberation of an 'activist' who is in gaol for attempting to assassinate a Prime Minister or for blowing up a police station in an Asian or Western country. But, as Aristotle wrote to distinguish is the mark of the human intelligence; and of human honesty too.

When we speak of prisoners of conscience, surely we can so distinguish between the bomb-thrower in a South American jail and the dissident philosopher in the Serbsky Institute. We can scarcely object to the arrest of Lieutenant Ilyin, who attempted to assassinate Mr. Brezhnev a few years ago, though the fact that nothing has been said of his fate raises other questions. At any rate, he is in a different class from the brave and unfortunate Soviet citizens who formed a committee to check on Soviet observance of the Helsinki agreement, almost all of whom have been jailed as if to prove that their doubts were correct.

We can, surely, distinguish too between violence used as a method of preserving rule, and violence which is a method of rule in itself. That is to say, there are cases in which a limited number of political opponents are unjustly and inhumanely treated, are gaoled or executed. And there is the institutionalization of this violence as the administrative method used against the population as a whole, which has always been found in systems of the Soviet type. This second, and greater, terror is especially associated with regimes whose principles involve intervening in the life of the people, not just to secure general political acquiescence, but to control their everyday behaviour in non-political fields. And, above all, it arises when the regime is devoted to 'social engineering'—that is, the destruction or total transformation of the way of life of entire social classes, as with the collectivization of the peasantry in the USSR and later in Vietnam and elsewhere.

Traditionalist (or old-style military) regimes may treat their political opponents in the most barbarous fashion. But they seldom make huge social or racial groups the automatic targets of atrocity, or try to wrench the whole of society into new attitudes and enthusiasms; this is not easily achieved without a massive use of the execution cellar and the labour camp.

Do the media make these distinctions? I have not come

across figures for Britain, but would be surprised if they differed much from those found in the United States. There, in the year 1976, news stories, editorials, and signed opinion on violations of human rights in *The New York Times*, *The Washington Post*, and the three leading television news shows numbered 137 stories on Chile and 7 on Cuba, 90 on South Korea and one on North Korea—while Cambodia rated 16 stories . . .

The hostile propaganda machine is efficient not only in spreading 'atrocity' stories but also other distorted views which we do not rebut sufficiently. It is quite extraordinary how the misleading propaganda phrases of our opponents are left unchallenged. The idea that the neutron bomb's role is to 'kill people without harming property' is quite pervasive. The fact that it actually kills fewer people than tactical Soviet nuclear weapons is forgotten. So is its real purpose—to kill tank crews. It is widely described and accepted as a 'capitalist' weapon, with people's lives being readily expendable and property sacrosanct. (One can think of other weapons which kill people and do little harm to buildings—bullets, for instance.) Mr. Callaghan did give this argument short shrift, but in the Netherlands and elsewhere the ploy had its effect. It is of course a hoary tradition for propagandists to condemn weapons which the other side has and they do not have. During the First World War the Allies condemned German submarine warfare and the Germans attacked the inhumanity of the blockade. More recently the United States was attacked for dropping bombs from the air in Vietnam, while critics failed to condemn high explosives lobbed into Saigon by mortar or planted to explode in its restaurants. In the case of the neutron bomb we simply did not conduct the defensive and counteroffensive high level propaganda battle which was needed to establish the relevant truth.

In America and elsewhere it is common to read of the 'British Army' in Northern Ireland, with the implication that it is a force imposed from outside. But except as a convenient shorthand, there is no such organization. There is Her Majesty's

Army, the army of the United Kingdom, including famous Northern Irish regiments. It fights under the flag of the United Kingdom with its Cross of St. Patrick. The stars of its officers carry the phrase 'Tria Juncta in Uno'.

In the case of Rhodesia, the 'front line states' are often described as those 'bordering on' Rhodesia; neither Tanzania nor Angola do so, and both Zaire and Malawi are closer than the other two, but their voices are not heard since neither of them cares to serve as a training ground in the handling of Soviet weapons.

There is also a much cherished myth that Allende's government was 'democratically elected'. It was not. His vote was little over a third of the whole, and constitutionally inadequate. The election was thrown open to the Congress, and the Christian Democrats finally gave Allende their vote on receiving a guarantee that he would act constitutionally. As he told Régis Debray, he never had any intention of keeping this promise, and he was later censured by the Congress majority in very strong terms for breaches of the Constitution (and the Supreme Court also held this view). Needless to say, the overthrow of the Allende regime has been explained very simply in propagandist circles as the work of the CIA, which so wickedly helped to finance opposition newspapers and strike committees, while the North Koreans were giving arms and weapon training to the left-wing terror squads.

Anti-Western demonology has made much of the CIA. Perhaps an analysis of this attitude by a Belgrade newspaper may carry more weight than the mere presentation of obvious facts. *Borba* (October 31, 1967), the official Yugoslav Communist organ, commented at length and in detail during an anti-CAI scare there:

Among all the information and stories circulating the country, especially recently, there are many which insist that many of our problems and difficulties are either inspired, or directly created by the CIA's activity. Thus, for example, stories can be heard to the effect that CIA caused the fires in 'Tudor Durkin', Belgrade, and in RIZ and 'Radio Koncar', Zagreb; that it was responsible for the fire aboard the 'Trebinje', that it caused the row in Niš-Ekspres, as well as the work stoppage in the shipyard 'Uljanik' in Pula, that it had its fingers in Rajakovic's escape from Piran,

that of all things, it persuaded the late Boris Krajger to become
its agent, and that it was the CIA which, by various methods,
created a split in our leading political organs . . . and many,
many other things.

However, when the sources and objectives of this kind of
'confidential' information are studied more closely, and when
we analyse them more thoroughly, it will not be difficult for us
to find that the 'CIA obsession' is being spread and encouraged
in our country by the vestiges of the class enemy, by the reac-
tionary, and especially, the bureaucratic and now powerless
forces, which oppose both the reform and the decisions of the
Fourth Plenum of the Central Committee as well as our
development in general [that is to say, by the agents of the
Soviet Union R.C.]. It is easy enough to identify them and see
their intentions. It is perfectly well known from which circles,
from which sides they stem.

Boris Krajger, the economic reformist Vice Premier, died
in a car crash in December 1966. The rumour about him—(see
Politika, 10 October 1967)—was that he had left $40,000–
$50,000 from the CIA deposited in a Swiss bank.

Borba went on to say:

These rumours are being spread by forces which, by compromising Krajger, and by presenting him as a CIA agent, are actually
wishing to compromise all his collaborators, all who share his
views, as well as the entire reform. They thus wish to bring confusion and distrust among the citizens and members of the
League of Communists.

Borba also said that stories had been put about that the CIA
was guilty of certain cases of arson, but that the truth appeared
to be 'that individual enterprises wish to rid themselves of
excessive stocks by 'selling' the burnt goods to the insurance
company'.

This Communist view—and especially the point that CIA
mania usually proceeds from agents of the Soviet clandestine
services—might be taken to heart by certain Western witch-
hunters, and remind us that a reasonable foreign policy must
also include a serious attack on the problem of Soviet and
Eastern European espionage and subversion. The most obvious
action is to insist that these countries should not maintain

staffs in London larger than we have in their own capitals. The usual estimate of full-time KGB and GRU agents in Soviet embassies and trade delegations is around forty percent; we do not need them. We should seek common policy on this with all members of the Western alliance, and hope that such an example might be followed by Third World countries, most of whom have had the same problem. Like most elements in a sound policy, such action would also be very popular in the UK—as was shown by the fact that the expulsion of over a hundred Soviet spies under the last Conservative government was followed by opinion polls showing higher approval than they had done for any government act for over a decade.

When Britain asked the USSR to help trace the way in which Soviet arms got to the IRA, that assistance was not forthcoming. Suspicious circumstances, such as the interception of a planeload of arms from Czechoslovakia in Amsterdam, may be taken as *prima facie* evidence that there was a conscious Soviet involvement. This sort of thing should not be left to die down harmlessly.

Weakness on such matters is bound up with a generally weak attitude to negotiation as a whole. The Soviet Union has the advantage that it can work on the Western public and thus bring certain pressures to bear on the Western governments in a way which does not happen the other way around. They are often in a position to say in effect: 'If you don't accept our terms, you won't get any agreement at all'. The desire of part of the Western public for at least the appearance of agreement— the perennial weakness of peaceable nations from the times of Ethelred the Unready to Neville Chamberlain—may put a serious pressure on the Western government concerned. There is a constant temptation to settle for worthless or even dangerous terms.

While one school of thought in the West holds that the Soviet Union is not dangerously strong nor likely to become so, there is another which believes that Soviet emergence as the leading military power, exerting its influence energetically throughout the world, could not be avoided. Gibbon comments on the failure of the West to do anything effective to prevent the capture of Constantinople by the Turks in 1453 (which had it succeeded would have provided a permanent and powerful base in the rear of the forthcoming invasions). He remarks on the weakness of some states, the remoteness of others, and adds, 'By some, the danger was considered as imaginary, by others, as inevitable'.

These destructive moods and arguments may only apply to a small minority, and they may convince only a very few more of those who hear them, and yet, even if they do not prevail they nevertheless exert an influence and pervade a currently uncertain atmosphere, so that the saner members of the population may feel some erosion of the clarity of their convictions. For this reason, a sound foreign policy must involve firm and outspoken leadership at home. At present the attitude of the representatives of the patriotic majority is defensive, this must change and the fight must be carried to the partisans of defeat.

There is a long record of Westerners, who have been duped who for one or another reason have radically misunderstood the Soviet leadership. Many have been disillusioned by some particularly striking Soviet act—from the Kronstadt Rising to the Hungarian Revolution or the invasion of Czechoslovakia. But many are not, others are only temporarily awakened, and there are always new generations of recruits.

The West, democracy, and peace have all suffered much from these delusions. But hitherto our survival has not been at risk. We have now reached a point where we simply cannot afford any more mistakes. There is no leeway. For all of us in the West, the next time is likely to be 'for real', as the Americans say. The situation is not hopeless so long as reasonable policies are pursued. The danger is that they may not be that, after all, we will not nerve ourselves to master the challenges of the next decade, and find ourselves instead having to say:

Time and again were we warned of the dyke, time and again we delayed:
Now, it may fall, we have slain our sons, as our fathers we have betrayed'.

Index